CODEPENDENCY NO MORE AND BUILD SELF-ESTEEM NOW

How You Can Be Codependent No More, Overcome Fear of Abandonment and Feel Better About Yourself

How to Feel Secure, Be Confident and Fearless, and Start Caring for Yourself

SARAH P. COEN

TABLE OF CONTENTS

INTRODUCTION

Let me start this book by telling you why I wanted to write this book on codependency. My childhood was not an easy one at all. My father was an alcoholic and also a sex addict. And my mother was a codependent spouse. He used my mother to the point of being abusive, and even as I child, when I did not the technical terms like codependency and abusiveness, I knew something was not right.

Not only because my father's behavior affected the family badly, but also because my mother would appease him instead of ticking him off. I learned later on that my family was dysfunctional because of my parents' relationship with each other. Let me give you a few examples of my parents' interactions with each other.

My father would come home drunk and beat my mother with his belt. She would have bruises all over her body. She would cry, of course, cry and tell him to stop. But nothing more than that. When the bout of abuse was done, she would get up and go and console my father instead of the other around!

"I'm so sorry, my dear. Why are you so angry? Did I do anything wrong?" she would plead with him.

"Yes, the lunch you sent me today was horrible. My friends mocked me because I have a wife who can't even cook!" He would reply. Often, it would be reasons as frivolous as this.

"I'm sorry. I will improve my cooking skills, okay? Would that be fine?" Again, my mother would plead.

Such instances were common during my growing-up years. Not only would my mother not fight back with my dad for the injustices he heaped on her, but also treat him like a king. As a teenager, I would ask her, "Why are you not doing anything about the way dad is treating you? He uses abusive language, hits you, throws the food you cooked in the bin because he thinks it's not good, and even puts lighted cigarette butts on your body. And yet, you behave like as if it is your fault, he is doing whatever he is doing."

She would reply, "No, no, you don't understand, my dear. I need him in my life. Without him, I would not know how to live. He brings money so that we can put food on the table. He provides for us. We need him. These inconveniences are a small price to pay."

I remember being quite surprised by her reply. So, what if he is providing for us? I would think to myself, "Every family member has a role to play, and his role is to provide for us. And why didn't I feel the same way about my dad? Why did I hate him for what he is doing instead of thinking like my mother?"

These questions not only baffled me but also drove me to dig deeper into psychology, a subject I loved a lot. And slowly, I realized that my mother was actually in a codependent relationship. She believed she needed her husband badly. She thought that if she stood up to him and question his attitude, then he would leave her, and she would not be able to handle herself.

I thought it is time now to put the lessons I have learned in my life into a book so that others can benefit from them. Moreover, considering I am a self-help expert, it made sense to write a book on this subject. So, what is codependency? To get a better idea and to see if you are in a codependent relationship, find answers to the following questions:

Have you spent a lot of your time trying to meet the needs of your partner? Do you find trapped in your relationship? Are you always the one making sacrifices in your relationship? If you answered yes, then you are in a codependent relationship. The term codependency was introduced a few decades ago, but the definition has changed over the years.

Codependency is a psychological disorder prevalent in people from dysfunctional families. People in one-sided relationships often develop codependent behavior since one person may rely heavily on their partner to meet their self-esteem and emotional needs. This disorder enables people to maintain addictive, underachieving, and irresponsible behavior.

Codependency is worrying because you will develop many other issues if you are codependent. You will also have low self-esteem, rely on negative self-talk, and develop an inferiority complex if you are codependent. This book provides information about these issues and also provides you tips to help overcome these issues. If you have these issues and are codependent, there is a good chance you will stop caring about your needs and feelings. This is a horrible thing to do because you forget your importance. The book will make it easier and give you some tips you can use to care more for yourself.

Most people do not understand what codependency is, and because of this, there are many myths about this disorder. The symptoms and effects associated with this disorder are a little difficult to understand, but after reading through this book, you will gain a clearer understanding. It is important to note that codependency is a learned behavior, and most people develop these characteristics or traits as children. If you display any such traits, you need to control them before they harm you and your loved one.

If you are codependent, you may have low self-esteem, and self-care will not be a priority. Since caring for others is what gives you happiness, you stick to your partner no matter how abusive he/she may be. You do this because you fear abandonment and loneliness. If you are alone, you may use alcohol or drugs to comfort you. This behavior affects your life, and you find yourself losing control. So, you try to gain control by telling those close to you how they should behave.

In the course of this book, you will learn everything you need to know about codependency as well as various codependent behaviors. The book provides information about the myths and facts about codependency and helps you determine how you can assess if you are codependent. You will also gather information about the treatment and recovery process of codependency.

Do you want to learn about all this? Are you eager to improve your life and mold it according to your desires? If yes, this book will act as your guide every step of the way. If you are excited to discover the secrets to doing this, let's get started immediately!

CHAPTER ONE

AN INTRODUCTION TO CODEPENDENCY

Codependency is a behavior people learn, and it's a trait passed on from one generation to the next. Codependency is a behavioral and emotional condition that affects a person's ability to develop and maintain a healthy and mutually satisfying relationship. This behavior is also known as relationship addiction since a person with codependency often develops and maintains one-sided relationships. They may also find themselves in abusive or destructive relationships.

Psychologists identified this disorder a decade ago when they studied different forms of interpersonal relationships in numerous alcoholic families. When different family members display codependent behavior, it becomes a learned behavior by watching, imitating, and mirroring the behavior.

WHO IS AFFECTED BY CODEPENDENCY?

Since codependency is a learned behavior, it can affect anybody, including a parent, sibling, spouse, co-worker, or friend of a person who is addicted to drugs or alcohol. The term codependent was first used to describe someone who was chemically dependent or someone who was in a relationship with an addict. Now, because psychologists have seen similar patterns in people who live with people with mental illnesses, the term codependency has also broadened to describe people from odd or dysfunctional families who are deemed codependent.

DYSFUNCTIONAL FAMILIES AND CODEPENDENCY

I am sure you may have come across many dysfunctional families. So, how would you define a dysfunctional family? Would it be one suffering from anger? Pain? Shame? Fear? Well, it could be one or all of them. A dysfunctional family is one where some members of the family feel denied or ignored. Some of the underlying problems include:

- Existence of sexual, emotional, or physical abuse
- A family member's addiction to alcohol, drugs, abusive relationships, food, gambling, sex, or any other activity
- A member suffering from chronic physical or mental illness

Any or all of the above factors can cause discord in a family. A dysfunctional family will never acknowledge that a problem exists between the members of the family. Most members choose to ignore the problem or avoid talking about it, and that can cause most family members to repress their emotions and forget about their wants or needs. The members of such families are often termed as survivors, and they develop behaviors that prevent them from considering their own needs. They also do their best to avoid difficult emotions and pretend to be happy. They numb their pain and detach themselves from the people around them. They never confront, talk, touch, trust, feel, or sense any emotion. The emotional development and identity development of the members of any dysfunctional family are inhibited.

Every codependent person needs someone to take care of. They focus their energy and attention solely on taking care of the unwell or sick person. A codependent person does not focus on their emotions, needs, and feelings but chooses to care only for another person's health, safety, and welfare.

An example of a codependent person is Adora Crellin from the show "Sharp Objects." The protagonist of the show, Camille Preaker, lives away from her mother, Adora, for a long time. When she comes home, she notices that her mother goes to the absolute limits to make sure her younger sister Amma constantly needs their mother. The mother even feeds Amma rat poison every day and gives her large doses on days when she feels a strong urge to care for someone. She does this to feed off the attention of Amma. This is a classic example of severe codependent behavior.

Examples

Codependent people do not have bad intentions unless they try to manipulate others. They only want to take care of the people around them. They want to care for their family members who are struggling in life. Since they cannot control their emotions, their actions become unhealthy and compulsive. Their attempts to save, support, and rescue the people around them make it easier for the other individuals to depend too much on them.

My mother thought she was protecting my siblings and me from losing the support of our father, both financially and emotionally. She took the abuses upon herself because she thought she needed to sacrifice herself for the sake of her children. This helped her feel vindicated about her irrationally submissive behavior.

If you are codependent, the act of giving often satisfies you since you are being recognized. Some of your choices may backfire, and you may grow resentful or feel trapped. This makes you feel helpless, but you cannot break away from that person. It also becomes hard for you to change the way you interact with the person. This relationship but deteriorates over time. It will be riddled with frustration, pity, and anxiety. There is no comfort or love in the relationship.

For some codependents, such relationships are common. They look for relationships or friendships where they always look like martyrs. Since they always focus on taking care of the other person, they lose sight of everything that they want or need and are often hailed for their sacrifices.

There are different forms of codependency; we will look at some of these in further detail later in the chapter.

Let us now look at examples of codependent relationships.

PARENTS AND CHILDREN

Example 1:

Parents usually try to clean up after their children, and they do this even after the child has reached his teens. Let us assume that you have a child who has moved back home. Apart from cleaning up after him, you also give him money so he can manage his daily affairs. You do not speak to your child about the fact that he does not have a job or even ask him how he spends his money. You may be doing this because you do not want to offend or upset your child. When you give your child money and care for him, you feel a sense of purpose and meaning.

This is what happened with Carol and her son, Ivan. Ivan worked for a while after finishing his college education, but thanks to a recession in his industry, he lost his job and returned home to be with his mother until he could get another job. Carol felt sad for her son and believed it was her responsibility to provide for him until he found a job.

She gave him food, clothing, and shelter for more than six months. Now, what happened was that Ivan got used to his easy life, to find his needs met without having to work for it. In fact, he used emotional blackmail to take money from his mother, even for partying and having fun with friends.

Carol kept telling herself that she was his mother, and if she did not help him, who will? Weeks turned to month, and months turned to years. Ivan had stopped trying to get a job, and Carol unwittingly got into a codependent relationship with her son. She was trapped, even though she was the one who was the provider.

Example 2:

Let us assume you are raising a visually or mentally challenged child. You do everything for your child because you think that is what you should do as a responsible parent of a child with special needs. There are things your child can learn and do for himself. But since your child is completely dependent on you for everything, you think you can do it all and never ask him to try anything on his own. You believe you are the only person who can assist your child.

Such classic examples of parents becoming codependent on their children are common. Parents get so attached to their differently abled children that they lose their own identity. Their children become their identity, and they get lost in a codependent relationship.

Example 3:

You are very close to your mother, and you do everything in your power to make her feel happy. If she has a bad day and calls you, you drop everything you are doing to make her feel better. You believe it is your job to care for your mother because you know why or how she feels this way. You think you are the only one who can help your mother feel better. You never leave town or spend too much time with the people around you because you believe your mother may need you. This will only make it harder for you to be in other relationships.

ROMANTIC RELATIONSHIPS

Example 1:

Let us assume your partner is an alcoholic. If he wakes up with a hangover, he cannot go to work. You may find ways to cover up for him by calling work and telling them that your partner is sick. You also call in sick at work because you want to take care of him. You never go out with your friends because he may go out for a drink and eventually need you. You go everywhere with him because you worry about him driving back home after drinking. You stop meeting your family because you feel embarrassed by how your partner behaves in front of them. You cannot confront him because you are afraid of how he may react.

Example 2:

Your partner has a chronic illness, and you do everything in your power to take care of him. He may have mobility issues, and the physician says that he needs to follow a specific diet. You feel sorry for your partner and do whatever you can to take care of him. If your partner says he doesn't like eating specific food on the diet plan, you ignore the plan and give him what he wants. You also discourage him from moving around because he should not be performing too much activity. You do everything in your power to care for his needs.

In each of the examples provided, the codependent person has multiple ways out of the situation, but the fear of losing the other person drives them to either ignore or pretend these solutions do not exist. An individual in a codependent relationship gets inextricably tied to it, not because of the other person but because of his or her own misplaced sense of need.

TYPES OF CODEPENDENCY

Relationships Involving Abuse

When you are in an abusive relationship, there is an imbalance, especially when it comes to power, in the relationship. Since the abuse is not continuous, you believe that the relationship is not too bad. You may develop or identify some patterns to make sure your partner does not get upset. This increases the number of secrets you keep from your partner and the people around you. This means the relationship will only be superficial since you cannot be intimate with your partner. You also feel ashamed for being in such a relationship.

This is what happened to my mother. There were times when my father could be quite loving and compassionate and take us out on family picnics and other fun activities. He would buy expensive gifts for my mother too, sometimes. Maybe it was his way of saying sorry to her, but the abuses never stopped.

Whenever I tried reasoning with my mother about her relationship with my dad, she would take examples from these on-and-off good times and say, "Remember he bought those beautiful earrings for me on my birthday. If he did not love me, would he have done so? Your father is okay. Just sometimes, he loses his temper, and I think I am to blame for most of his problems. I need to take better care of him now."

Relationships Involving Addiction

When your partner is addicted, it creates a sense of infidelity. There is something other than you that takes a primary space in your relationship. If your partner hides their addiction from you, then you will likely feel a sense of betrayal and grow upset once you find out. There is a lot of threatening, promising, pleading, silence, lying, and other communication patterns in your relationship. You begin to accommodate your schedule and habits according to them, so you can maintain a sense of order. Since addiction is a habit, the accommodations you make become unhealthy for you.

A friend of mine, Anita (name changed for privacy), was in a live-in codependent relationship with a drug addict. She was so attached to him that she would never come out for parties with us because she was scared that he would get angry at her behavior and take more drugs as a way of punishing her. Anita lost many of her friends because she refused to keep in touch with them to accommodate her partner's life schedule.

In fact, Anita did not even tell her partner's parents about his problem. She would make excuses for his absence during family gatherings and parties. She would say, "Oh! He could not come today because he is working on a deadline." Or "He is sick and couldn't get up from bed," and other such reasons.

Soon, she had problems at work because she used to call in sick to be there for her partner. She ended up isolated herself from her friends and family because she believed she couldn't live without her partner and that it was her duty to protect him.

Relationships Involving Fear

If you only care to gain approval from the people around you, the Bible says that you have a fear of man and no fear of God. The first two forms of codependency we have looked at are due to fear and suffering; this form of codependency is based on your choices and values. It is often called different things, including insecurity and peer pressure. If you have this form of codependency, you do whatever you can to please the people around you.

The reason we discussed the types of codependency is so you know them all, which can help you understand your behavior patterns and identify if you or someone you know is codependent.

CHARACTERISTICS OR BEHAVIOR

Codependent people often have low self-esteem and don't value themselves. They will do everything in their power to treat themselves as a second fiddle in comparison to the other people in their life. This is a voluntary character trait, and they also feel pity for themselves since they feel they are burdened by their behavior. Some codependents do try to change the way they feel by using nicotine, alcohol, or drugs. Since they do not know how to use them in moderation, they become addicted to them. Some people tend to gamble, indulge in indiscriminate sexual activity, work too hard, or develop other compulsive behaviors.

These people have good intentions, and they do their best to care for the people around them. They want to do everything in their power to care for those who experience difficulties, but their caretaking becomes defeating and compulsive. Some commonly seen examples of such behavior are:

- A husband/wife may make excuses for their partner's unavailability
- A mother/father may support their child regardless of their behavior and make excuses
- A mother/father may use her/his power to pull strings to make sure their children do not suffer from the consequences of their behavior

The trouble is that these repeated rescue attempts make the needy individual continue to depend on the person which leads to a destructive path for both parties involved. They believe the person taking care of them is their benefactor and will develop an unhealthy need to be around them.

When this reliance increases, the codependent will develop a sense of satisfaction and reward when they know they are needed. The mother in the show "Sharp Objects" always wanted to be needed by her children. She did everything she could to make sure they wanted to be taken care of by her. When the codependent focuses on being needed, his behavior becomes compulsive, which makes him feel helpless or choiceless in his relationship. Though he knows how he feels, he cannot break away from this cycle. A codependent always views himself as a victim, and he is often attracted to the same weakness in friendship and love relationships.

CHARACTERISTICS OF CODEPENDENT PEOPLE

- Dishonesty/lying
- Chronic anger
- Stress
- Lack of self-trust or trust in others
- Difficulty in making decisions
- Poor communication methods
- Difficulty identifying emotions and feelings
- The trouble with boundaries and intimacy
- Fear of being alone or abandoned
- Inability to adapt to change
- The need to control the situation and the people around them
- A tendency to be upset or hurt when people do not recognize or understand their efforts
- The need to always do more than what is needed or expected of them
- A sense of responsibility towards the actions performed by people around them

- A tendency to confuse pity and love with the tendency to always love the people around them whom they can rescue or pity
- A sense of guilt when they need to assert themselves
- A need to be recognized and approved
- A dependence on different types of relationships. They will do everything in their power to avoid feeling lonely or abandoned.

SYMPTOMS OF CODEPENDENCY

Have you noticed that you expend your energy to meet the needs of everybody around you? Do you find yourself trapped in a relationship? Are you making too many sacrifices in your relationship? If you said yes to even one of the above questions, you are in a codependent relationship.

Psychologists found that the symptoms of codependency often get worse when you don't treat them. The advantage is that it is easy to treat these symptoms since they are reversible. The following contains some symptoms of codependents and people in a codependent relationship. It is important to understand that you do not have to have all these symptoms for you to be codependent.

Low Self-Esteem

When you feel you are not good enough and often compare yourself to the people around you, you have low self-esteem. The trouble with self-esteem is that most people think very highly of themselves. Still, this is only a disguise, and people behave this way when they feel inadequate or unloved. When trying to understand these feelings you will discover an underlying feeling of shame beneath everything you feel. Perfectionism and guilt are signs of low self-esteem. When everything in your life is perfect, you no longer feel bad about your habits or yourself.

People-Pleasing

You can please the people you care about. It is okay to do this. Though, codependents think they never have a choice. They cannot say no because that makes them feel incompetent, and that leads to anxiety. Some codependents cannot say no to anybody around them. They do everything in their power to sacrifice their needs, so they can accommodate the needs of the people around them.

No Boundaries

A boundary is a line that you draw between yourself and the people around you. This boundary determines what is yours and what is not. This boundary applies to everything, including money, body, belonging, emotions, thoughts, needs, and feelings. It is difficult for codependents to draw the line when it comes to their emotions, feelings, thoughts, and needs.

A codependent does not have strong boundaries. If you are codependent, you always find yourself feeling responsible for other people's problems and feelings. It is extremely easy for you to blame yourself for their failures. Some codependents often have very rigid boundaries, and they are often withdrawn or closed off. This makes it extremely hard for people to get close to them. People often flip back and forth between having rigid and weak boundaries.

React

One of the troubles with codependency is that you will react to a person's feelings or thoughts. If you come across someone who says something you do not agree with, you will either become defensive or believe what he or she has to say. You tend to absorb another person's opinions since you do not have any boundaries. When you have a boundary, you realize that what they said was only their opinion and not a reflection of who you are or how you think.

Caretaking

Another issue with no proper boundaries is that if someone around you has a problem, you will do everything in your power to help them. You do not care about how you feel or what you need when you try to help them. It is natural for you to feel sympathy and empathy for the people around you, but you will tend to put that person ahead of yourself. You may have a strong urge to help another person and even feel rejected when that person does not want your help. You will try to help someone to help and fix.

Control

When you are in control, you feel secure and safe. If you are codependent, you want to control every aspect of your life because you cannot live with even a little uncertainty or chaos. You avoid taking risks because you need to live with certainty. It becomes difficult for you to share your thoughts and emotions. So, you steer clear of relationships with people and resort to comforting yourself through drugs or alcohol. You may also immerse yourself in work because you can control everything you do there.

As a codependent, you want to control every situation in your life. You want people to act a certain way, and you may convince them to do this by manipulating their emotions. You come off as bossy because you tell people to do things your way. Since they have no boundaries of their own, they forget about others' boundaries as well.

Inability to Communicate

If you are codependent, you do not communicate your thoughts, emotions, and feelings because you do not think they matter. So, you stop thinking about your thoughts and emotions, and this becomes a problem for you in the future. You know exactly how you feel, but never own up to those feelings for many reasons, including:

- Being afraid to tell people how you feel

- Not wanting to upset the people around you because you want to please them

If something is happening around you that you do not like, you refrain from telling them how you feel. You pretend everything is okay. Alternatively, you may also choose to control the situation because you are unable to tell people how you feel. In such instances, try to control the situation and change things to work in your favor by forcing the people around you to act the way you see fit. Since you cannot communicate why you are acting this way, they do not understand what you are going through, and steer clear of you.

Obsessive Behavior

Codependents never give themselves a thought. It is always about the people around them. They do everything they can to make sure the people around them are taken care of. A codependent does this because of his fears, dependencies, and anxieties. He also wants things around him to be perfect and becomes obsessed with the idea of perfectionism. He may spend a lot of time fantasizing about how a situation can turn out. Since most codependents are afraid of being alone, they stick to any relationship they are in, regardless of how abusive it may be. They may also fantasize about being in a relationship with someone and may become obsessed with them.

Dependent on Others' Opinions

Codependents want the people around them to like them. This is the only way they can feel good about themselves. Some codependents want to be in a relationship because they never want to be alone. They fear abandonment and loneliness if they are alone for too long. This characteristic makes it difficult for them to end relationships, even abusive or painful relationships.

Denial

Most codependents cannot accept what they are going through. They never want to face their problems. They try to find problems in the situation or other people, so they keep complaining or try to fix the people around them. They may also move from one relationship to another, but don't agree that they are the problem. A codependent also denies his needs and feelings.

If you are codependent, you do push your feelings at the back and tend to focus on the feelings of the people around you. You also pay more attention to the needs of the people around you and not to yourself. They do not try to reach the people around them for help, as they cannot accept the fact that they needed another person's help. This is only true for those people who pretend to be self-sufficient. Some codependents are needy. Since they cannot communicate what they are going through, they control the situation or become obsessed with the people around them.

Trouble with Intimacy

When I talk about intimacy, I am not referring to physical intimacy. Having said that, sexual dysfunction is often a clear sign of troubles with intimacy. When I say intimacy, I mean, how open, or close you are with the people around you; you fear that the people around you will reject, leave, or judge you. You also have trouble being in a relationship since you are worried about being smothered. You feel as though your partner takes up too much of your time, and you tend to deny your need to be close to someone. When you continue to do this, your partner will complain you never have time for him.

Pain

When you are codependent, it creates stress and often leads to a lot of pain. When you have low self-esteem and are ashamed of yourself, you become anxious about being rejected, abandoned, or judged. You never want to make mistakes and fear that a mistake will make you look like a failure. This will make you feel trapped, whether you are alone or with people. Some other symptoms of codependency lead to resentment, anger, hopelessness, despair, and depression. When the feelings become too much for you to deal with, you become numb.

There are different ways for you to recover and change the way you behave and think. It becomes difficult for you to identify a way to change your thoughts and behavior since the symptoms of codependency are habits that are ingrained in you. You can overcome codependency if you accept what you are going through. This is the hardest step. Once you are past this bump, you can find the right treatment method to help you overcome codependency.

We will look at different ways to treat these symptoms later in the book.

CHAPTER TWO

MYTHS AND FACTS

When it comes to codependency, people in a relationship find themselves interdependent. They cannot survive without the presence of each other. There are numerous myths surrounding codependency because not many people understand what codependency is. It is only when you know the facts that you will learn about it.

MYTH 1: ONLY RELATIONSHIPS INVOLVING ADDICTION CAN LEAD TO CODEPENDENCY

Fact: Codependency occurs in any relationship, and it is not limited to only those relationships where one person has an addiction. The term codependency was used in the past to describe relationships where one or both individuals had addictions. As mentioned earlier, this term has evolved since then to include any type of dysfunctional relationship. Codependent relationships can involve people with terminal conditions or mental illnesses.

Codependent relationships can exist between romantic partners, spouses, children, friends, colleagues, and other relationships. Codependent relationships are not limited only to those relationships where there is abuse or addiction. There are some cases where you may find yourself in a codependent relationship with someone who may be irresponsible. In this case, you may take up the responsibilities to pay bills, complete daily tasks, and maintain a job. In such relationships, you, as the codependent person, may derive self-esteem since your partner needs you.

To further understand codependency and establish that addiction does not have to be present in a relationship to become codependent, immense research was conducted. A study conducted by Knudson T. et al. (2012) showed that people who grew up in a dysfunctional family were usually codependent in the future. They didn't find that addiction could lead to codependency. This study concludes that codependency does not only occur in those individuals with addiction.

MYTH 2: CODEPENDENCY IS A MENTAL HEALTH DISORDER

Fact: It is important to note that codependency is not a mental health disorder, and it cannot be diagnosed. You cannot expect a mental health professional to determine if you have codependency or not. It is not a condition recognized by clinical psychologists and is not listed down in the Diagnostic and Statistical Manual of Mental Disorders.

Codependency describes the different types of relationships and represents different behavioral patterns but is not a mental health disorder. Some mental health professionals and experts believe that codependency should be considered a disorder, even though it is not diagnosable. There are various assessment tools you can use to determine if you experience codependency. For instance, you can use the Codependency Assessment Tool, which measures different factors, such as neglect of self, low self-esteem, and low self-worth. You can also use the questions in the next chapter to determine if you are codependent.

MYTH 3: CODEPENDENCY IS THE SAME THING AS BEING CLINGY

Fact: Being codependent is not only about displaying behaviors that make you clingy. It is more significant than that. A clingy person wants to spend time with his significant other. When you are codependent, you want to do more than just spend time with your significant other. You will want to care obsessively for your significant other if you are in a codependent relationship. You also take an excessive amount of care and responsibility when it comes to your significant other. Codependent people often forget about their wants and needs because they want to care for the other person in the relationship.

Codependency is different from clinginess in the sense that people in codependent relationships rely only on the relationship to maintain self-esteem and happiness. A codependent will do everything in his power to prevent the relationship from ending. He hates the feeling of loneliness and abandonment and will try to save the relationship even if it becomes unhealthy.

MYTH 4: YOU ARE CODEPENDENT, OR YOU ARE NOT

Fact: Some people may demonstrate some characteristics of codependency when compared to others. As mentioned earlier, codependency is not an official mental health disorder. So, there is no one standard you can use to determine how codependent an individual may be other than life experiences. There is a co-dependency spectrum that helps you determine if you are codependent or not. One end of the spectrum indicates no codependency while the opposite end marks severe codependency, and anything in between the ends is considered mild or moderate codependency.

A person with low levels of codependency may choose to put the needs of others over theirs occasionally. They may also try to fix a person's problems if needed. Alternatively, people who display severe codependency behaviors need to take care of the people around them. They do their best to rescue them from any issue or trouble they find themselves in. When it comes to mild and severe codependency, people may display some codependent behaviors.

MYTH 5: CODEPENDENT PEOPLE ARE IMMATURE AND WEAK

Fact: People who experience codependency often have troubled family relationships. People who have grown up in a dysfunctional family tend to demonstrate various codependent behaviors as they grow up. Additionally, many people learn various codependent behaviors from their families. They also repeat these behaviors in their relationships. It is important to understand that a codependent person is neither immature nor weak. They only engage in some codependent behaviors since they have always watched people behave this way.

There is enough evidence to prove that a person who has experienced physical abuse, emotional abuse, or emotional neglect during their childhood becomes more codependent in the future. Thus, codependency is not a sign of immaturity or weakness. It is a way for a person to cope with the effects of any childhood trauma or emotional needs.

MYTH 6: YOU CANNOT OVERCOME CODEPENDENCY

Fact: It is possible to change codependent behavior, and there are different forms of therapy you can use to do this. Through treatment, you can correct dysfunctional behaviors, so you enjoy different healthy relationships. When you try to treat codependency, you can explore the different behaviors you witnessed during childhood. This helps you determine how these behaviors made you develop unhealthy habits to cope with the trauma.

Research shows that people can overcome codependent behaviors if they want to enjoy healthy relationships. A study conducted by Bryne M. et al. (2008) shows that a 12-week group therapy treatment program helped people with codependency issues address various problems they had with their families and friends. This study also showed that the therapy session made it easier for people to overcome various mental health disorders, such as anxiety and depression.

CHAPTER THREE

ASSESSMENT AND TREATMENT

You cannot expect to understand if you are codependent or not through a brain scan or a simple lab test. There are different assessment tools you can use to help determine this, and you can meet with a mental health professional to understand them. In this assessment, you need to answer questions across five domains:

1. Self-neglect or other focus
2. Hiding your true self
3. Low self-esteem
4. Family with these issues
5. Medical problems

Let us look at each of the five domains in a bit of detail.

Self-Neglect - Self-neglect happens when you are so focused on what others think about you or how others perceive you that you totally ignore your own needs, desires, likes, and dislikes. You tend to worry so much about others, that you often forget to take care of yourself in a healthy manner.

For example, you binge eat, or forget to eat at all. Perhaps you eat things that are quick and might not be the most nutritious choices for your body. You've also stopped going to the gym or getting regular exercise and sleep. Your relationship has taken over your mind and all of your energy. You just don't find the time or the energy to take care of yourself while in the grip of codependency.

Alternatively, you could have had excellent skills, like writing or painting, or something creative. But now you do not spend time on these activities because you are excessively focused on the other person.

Is there something you really want to do for yourself, but you just can't because of the relationship you are in? If the answer is yes, then this is a clear sign of codependence and self-neglect.

Hiding Your True Self –

When in a codependent relationship, you are likely to hide your true self and project a personality for the sake of the other person. Let us take the example of Carol and her son, Ivan, who had returned home after he lost his job. Now, Carol would have been a person who loved to travel and have fun, but just to make her feelings similar to those of her son's, she might choose to say that she doesn't go out much so that she can be there for him.

Are you becoming a different person just to "fit in" to the relationship? If yes, then perhaps you need to delve deep and see if your authentic self is hidden behind layers of pretenses to keep the other person happy at all times.

- Low self-esteem - Here are clear signs of low self-esteem:
- Difficulty in speaking about your needs, priorities, and problems.
- Apologizing and feeling guilty often, many times, unnecessarily.
- Taking excessive care not to "rock the boat" in the relationship by keeping mum when you should have protested.
- Feeling unworthy or undeserving of the good things in life.
- Doing things for other people, especially for the other individual in the codependent relationship, more than you need to.
- Heeding your inner critical voice every time.

Families with Issues -

Here, I can give my own example. I come from a dysfunctional family, thanks to a codependent mom and an alcoholic and abusive dad. For people like me, it is easy to believe that being codependent was normal. In fact, I was lucky to have had a different mindset from that of my mother from an early stage, thanks to exposure to the outside world through books, friends, etc.

Ask yourself whether you come from a dysfunctional family. If yes, then you need to look at yourself, your behaviors, and attitudes more closely than otherwise to check if you have unwittingly carried forward these learned behaviors. And if you do recognize any symptoms of codependency in your personality, then it is time for you to take the bull by its horns.

Medical Problems -

Medical issues are one of the primary reasons individuals get caught in codependent issues. In a relationship, either of your medical problems, especially chronic cases, can lead to codependency. If you have an issue, then it may be possible that you are holding on to the other person for fear of losing them, and the reverse is also true. While it is a good thing, you are helping your partner, mother, adult child, etc., during their times of need, if you feel your life is not moving forward because of them, then it is time to do something about it.

The following are some statements used in the assessment that can help you determine if you are codependent or not.

1. I am compelled to help the people around me.
2. I have to control the events, so I know how to behave around people.
3. I am afraid to let people around me be who they want to be.
4. I cannot let the events happen naturally.
5. I am ashamed of my habits and behaviors.

6. I try to control people and events around me through guilt, helplessness, threats, coercion, manipulation, domination, or advice-giving.
7. I worry about having different medical problems.
8. I believe that my body is failing me, and so I tend to avoid handling problems.
9. I want to give people advice on what they need to do to solve their problems.
10. I believe my health, when compared to my family and friends, is deteriorating.
11. I always put on a happy face regardless of how I feel.
12. I always keep my thoughts, emotions, and feelings to myself and never let people know how I feel.
13. I am tired and feel ill.
14. I prevent people from learning about how I feel.
15. I do not talk to people about my thoughts and emotions.
16. Since my family did not talk about their problems when I was younger, I do not feel the same about speaking to the people around me.
17. I tend to have stomach issues.
18. I always pick on myself for everything. I think my feelings, looks, behavior, and actions cause too many problems.
19. I always push painful emotions and thoughts out of my awareness.
20. I grew up in a troubled or dysfunctional family.
21. My family always expressed their affections and feelings.

22. I am at fault for everything.
23. I am unhappy about how the people around me coped with different problems while I was growing up.
24. I am unhappy about how my family communicated with each other while we were growing up.
25. I feel embarrassed and humiliated.
26. I hate who I am.

Once you answer these statements, a mental health professional scores the assessment. It is only when you answer each question honestly will the professional make the right diagnosis.

TREATMENTS

Some people can overcome being codependent on their own. They read about codependency and learn everything there is to know about it. When they learn about how it harms people, it makes them want to change the way they behave. Others learn about their codependent nature through articles or books. Some stop being codependent when things change in their lives, such as when their partner finds a new job, learns to control his addiction, or does not require being cared for. In some cases, codependency requires some professional treatment. If you are codependent, you can use the following forms of treatment to change your behavior.

Group Therapy

You can consider different types of group interventions to treat codependency. The group dynamic gives you the chance to develop healthier and stronger relationships with the people around you. Since you are in a safe environment, you can be honest with each other about the relationship and your feelings. Through group therapy, you can hold the right individual accountable for a specific issue in the relationship. The methods of group therapy vary. Some of these forms include cognitive-behavioral therapy (CBT), where members learn more about their skills. Other group therapies use a 12-step model, where you learn about your symptoms and addictions. The objectives of these sessions can vary.

Family Therapy

Family therapy looks at the dynamics of a family, and each member needs to learn more about how their patterns and habits affect the relationships in the family. This form of therapy helps them learn more about how to improve the relationship. The goal of group therapy is to help the family improve communication. Family sessions may bring to light some issues that have never been discussed. Other times, individuals create change by getting sober or encouraging people to be more independent since that changes the family dynamic.

Cognitive Therapy

This form of therapy looks at people's thoughts and emotions. It determines how these thoughts and emotions contribute to various negative and unhealthy patterns in a relationship. For instance, if you are someone who thinks, "I cannot be alone," you will do everything in your power to maintain the relationship no matter how unhealthy it is for you to do so.

Cognitive therapy sessions focus on changing how you tolerate different emotions and thoughts. The objective of these sessions is to create a positive behavior change. This allows the people around you to accept responsibility for their actions and not blame you for everything that goes wrong. This form of treatment delves deep into your childhood since most people tend to develop codependent patterns when they see the people in their family behave this way. Through cognitive therapy, they will learn to get in touch with their emotions and help them experience different emotions and feelings again.

CHAPTER FOUR

RECOVERY

Most people make the mistake of believing that codependency is related to relationships. People believe that codependency is a disorder, which is not the case. We have discussed this in the second chapter where we looked at the different myths and facts associated with codependency. It is important to understand that you have the power to solve your problems, you don't really need others' help, except, perhaps, professional help to help you get the correct objective perspective of your state of mind and being. When you change your relationship with yourself, then the problem of codependency gets solved automatically.

The main issue with codependency is the reliance that you place on an individual, process, or substance. You may choose to gamble your problems away. You no longer have a healthy relationship with yourself, so you try to make something else or someone else more important. As time passes, your feelings, thoughts, actions, and emotions solely revolve around that one person, substance, or activity. Even without realizing it, you soon lose the ability to develop a relationship with yourself.

When it comes to recovering from codependent behaviors, you need to change the way you think and behave so you reconnect with yourself. You learn to honor yourself. When you heal or overcome codependent behaviors, you develop the following characteristics:

- Self-worth
- Authenticity
- Capability to be intimate
- Congruent and integrated thoughts, values, actions, and feelings

It is never easy to change, so it will take some time to commit to making the following changes:

REFRAINING FROM CODEPENDENT BEHAVIORS

This is the first step to overcome codependency. You need to make an effort to recover or refrain from showing codependent behaviors. The objective is to bring the attention back to you. You need to make sure you have internal control instead of external control. This means that you begin to act based on your values, morals, needs, emotions, and feelings. You no longer need another person's emotions and feelings to help you stay confident and calm. You learn to meet all your needs healthily. You don't need to refrain completely from displaying codependent behaviors. If you are a codependent person, you cannot refrain from showcasing some codependent behaviors. Since you depend and need other people to latch onto you, you compromise and constantly give in any relationship. You can learn to detach yourself from the people around you by practicing not controlling, obsessing, or trying to please the people around you. This is the only way you become more autonomous and self-directed.

If you are in a relationship with an addict or abuser or grew up as the child of an abusive parent, you will be afraid to please your significant other. You may need to display immense courage to break this pattern where you concede your power to another.

Being Aware

As mentioned earlier, a codependent person is always in denial. This is true, regardless of whether you come from a dysfunctional family, are in an abusive relationship, or have low self-esteem. Codependents find a way to deny their addictions and needs. They may be addicted to a person, drug, or activity. If you are a codependent person, you find the one thing most important to you, and this object takes precedence over your emotions, feelings, and needs.

You may have developed these codependent traits and behaviors because you grew up in a dysfunctional family or were not nurtured well by your parents. Nobody respected your feelings and opinions, and your emotional needs were never cared for. As the years went by, you learned to ignore your wants, needs, feelings, and emotions because you didn't want to risk criticism or rejection. Some people decide to find comfort in drugs, work, sex, and food.

This leads to low self-esteem. If you want to reverse these habits, you should learn to accept them. One of the many reasons why people develop low self-esteem is negative self-talk. People are never aware of the voices in their minds that criticize and push them to be better.

Accept the Emotions

When you want to heal, you need to accept yourself for who you are. This is not only a step in your recovery process, but it is a lifelong journey you need to take if you want to improve or change. People choose to undergo therapy because they believe it will help them change. You cannot overcome these behaviors if you do not accept yourself for who you are, and that can be a tough realization for some people.

Ironically, you should accept yourself for who you are if you want to change. You learn more about yourself during the recovery process. This is when you become mature. It is only when you accept the reality that you open the possibilities of change. New energy and ideas will emerge when you stop blaming yourself for everything. For instance, if you are upset, guilty, or lonely, do not let the emotions overwhelm you. This only makes it harder for you to control your stress and anxiety. Show yourself some compassion, soothe yourself, and take the necessary steps to help you improve.

When you accept yourself for who you are, you no longer feel the need to please the people around you. You no longer care about what others think about you. You learn to honor your wants and needs and learn to forgive yourself and the people around you. When you are nice to yourself, you learn to be self-reflective. You will no longer be self-critical. Your confidence and self-esteem grow, which means you do not allow people to tell you what to do or abuse you. You become more assertive and authentic.

Action

When you understand yourself better, you need to start acting. It is only through action that you grow. If you want to accept yourself, you need to change with new behavior. This means you need to take ventures and risks to help you improve. This may mean you need to speak up, go somewhere alone, set boundaries, or try something different.

When you act, it also means you need to set internal boundaries to help you commit to yourself. You need to learn to say no to yourself. When you do this, you learn to say no to the people around you. Never expect others to make you happy and meet your needs and wants. You should learn to act and meet your needs.

Do those activities that give you pleasure and satisfaction. Every time you try something new or take a new risk, you need to learn more about your feelings, needs, and emotions. This is the only way you learn more about yourself. When you learn to create a strong sense of who you are, your self-confidence and self-esteem improve. This helps you build a positive loop that safeguards against depression, low self-esteem, and fear.

It is important to understand that words also are actions. Everything you say about you has power over you. It reflects your self-esteem. When you become assertive, you learn to accept yourself for who you are. This is a powerful tool and step in your recovery process. If you want to be assertive, you need to know who you are and let the world know who you are, too. This is the only way you respect yourself. It is important to remember that you are the author of your life. It is not about what you do or how the people around you treat you.

CHAPTER FIVE

UNDERSTANDING SELF-ESTEEM

As mentioned earlier, if you are codependent, you may have low self-esteem, and this could be due to multiple reasons. If you want to overcome codependency, it is important to improve your self-esteem. Before we look at how you can do this, let us understand what self-esteem is.

People may have told you that confidence and self-esteem are two pillars of success. Low or no self-esteem often leaves people feeling depressed or defeated. They tend to make bad choices, fall into destructive relationships, and cannot live up to his or her potential. This does not mean you should have a grand sense of importance. High self-esteem can put people off and damage personal and professional relationships. If you think highly of yourself, it is an indication of narcissistic personality disorder.

Both excessively high and low self-esteem is bad for you and can cause harm. You need to strike a balance between the two. Develop a positive but realistic view of who you are. But where does self-esteem stem from?

INTRODUCTION TO SELF-ESTEEM

According to psychology, self-esteem is a term used to describe a person's sense of personal value or self-worth. In simple words, self-esteem helps you appreciate your worth. Through self-esteem, you can determine how much you like yourself. Self-esteem helps you understand how you perceive various aspects of yourself, such as your emotions, beliefs, behaviors, and appearance.

Many psychologists and theorists have written about self-esteem. Abraham Maslow, who wrote about the hierarchy of needs and developed the pyramid of self-actualization, described self-esteem as one of the main motivators for people to succeed. According to Maslow, a person can satisfy his needs and wants only when he learns to respect himself. He also needs people around him to accept him for who he is and motivate him to achieve his goals. It is only when this happens that he can grow as a person.

It is important to understand that self-esteem is different from self-efficacy. The latter is more about how you handle future performances, abilities, or actions, while the former is how you perceive yourself. This perception is what drives your success or failure.

IMPORTANCE OF SELF-ESTEEM

Self-esteem plays a significant role in motivating you and helping you succeed in life. If you have low self-esteem, you may hold yourself back from working up to your potential. Since you believe you are up to no good and cannot do anything in life, you do not do well in school or at work. You learn to navigate through every phase in life with an assertive and positive attitude when you have a healthy level of self-esteem. This attitude helps you accomplish your goals.

Here are some irrefutable benefits of building self-esteem, which is quite likely to spur you on to work on this key aspect of your personality.

You get to know and accept your authentic self - When your self-esteem is high; you are confident of your capabilities and live your life according to your needs and desires. Susan (name changed) was an amazing painter, but she was in an abusive, codependent relationship because of which her self-esteem was very low. And she did not believe in her skills.

When Susan was able to see how good she was at the work she did, she then found it easy to steer clear of toxic relationships and find the strength to move on with her life, on her terms. The lack of self-esteem makes you feel unworthy, which, in turn, makes you dependent on someone for your self-worth.

You learn to disagree and say no - One of the most common features of the lack of self-esteem is to accept everything and everyone around you as being right. Consequently, you end up feeling you know nothing, and you simply have to do what others tell you to.

As you build self-esteem, you see that others can also be wrong. This attitude teaches you to disagree when your limits are crossed and when you are taken for granted. You learn to say no when you should! And the best thing is, you find the courage and express your opinion and feelings without fear.

You feel confident to accept new challenges - Another common problem with codependency is that it becomes your comfort zone. You get so attached to the situation, even if it is not ideal, that you don't want to leave it because you fear anything new and unfamiliar. When your self-esteem is high, you find yourself overcoming the fear to try new challenges. And as you see, success in your new attempts, your self-esteem gets a bigger push.

All the above benefits directly impact your ability to handle yourself in such a way that you can break away from the shackles of codependency and create the life you truly deserve.

FACTORS THAT INFLUENCE SELF-ESTEEM

I am sure you know numerous factors influence self-esteem. Your age, thinking, potential illnesses, physical limitations, or disabilities are some factors that can affect your self-esteem. Your job and pay scale may also affect the way you think or perceive yourself. Some genetic factors help a person shape their personality, and if you have a parent with low self-esteem, you may also develop some of these characteristics. It is often your experiences that form the basis or core of your self-esteem. If you constantly receive negative or critical feedback from the people around you, you believe everything they say. This negative or critical feedback becomes the core of your self-esteem.

CHARACTERISTICS OF HEALTHY SELF-ESTEEM

The following are some characteristics to help you determine if you have a healthy self-esteem.

- You express your wants and needs
- You do not dwell on negative experiences or the past
- You are confident and have a positive approach to any situation
- You know when to say no to yourself and the people around you
- You know what your strengths and weaknesses are

CHARACTERISTICS OF LOW SELF-ESTEEM

You need to learn how to perceive yourself if you have the following problems:

- You believe people around you are better than you
- You focus on your weaknesses
- You cannot express your wants or needs comfortably
- You have a negative view of your life and cannot say no
- You are afraid of failure and experience different feelings, such as shame, anxiety, and depression
- You cannot accept positive feedback
- You struggle with being confident
- You put the needs of others before yours

CHAPTER SIX

CAUSES OF LOW SELF-ESTEEM

If you have low self-esteem, you need to take some time out of your schedule to determine what led you to believe you are up to no good. When you do this, you can determine some instances in your life that formed the basis of your self-esteem. You can also identify your strengths and weaknesses. Once you do this, you need to learn how to use your strengths to help you succeed. Yet, this is easier said than done. It is difficult to identify the causes of low self-esteem since every individual thinks differently. This chapter lists some reasons or factors that lead to low self-esteem. It is important to get familiar with them, so you can identify some causes in your life.

Negligent or Uninvolved Parents

As a child, you learn from the people around you. In most cases, the people around you influence your feelings about yourself. You begin to think of yourself in a specific way based on how people around you treat you. This is especially true when it comes to your guardians or parents.

Every individual needs to have a supportive and loving family, but some children are not as fortunate. Some children do not get the support they need from their parents because their parents suffer from different forms of addiction or mental health issues. Such parents cannot provide for their children or give them the love and support they need to grow.

If you have been in such a situation, you start believing that you can never be happy in life. You believe you do not deserve love or affection. You believe this because the people who should have taken care of you do not shower you with the love, affection, and care you deserve.

Peer Pressure or Negativity

The way you are treated by your guardians and parents significantly influences your self-esteem. Similarly, the way your peers behave around you or treat you affects your self-esteem.

If you are a part of a social group that brings you down, it will leave you feeling bad about yourself. They may force you to do things you do not want to do, not value your thoughts or emotions, or they may not respect you. This may make you feel like you are wrong. Your peers may also make you feel like you have to do what everybody else is doing or stick to what they say you can do. You stop listening to what you think is right. This damages the way you look at yourself.

Abuse

Trauma or abuse leads to feelings of guilt or shame, regardless of whether it is emotional, sexual, physical, or a combination of these. If you have faced trauma in the past, you may feel you deserve the abuse because of something you may have done in the past. You find yourself thinking you are not worth the other person's respect, love, or care. You may also suffer from depression and anxiety because of this abuse. This state of your mental health makes it difficult for you to lead a successful life.

Body Image

According to the University of Washington, over 53% of young girls are not happy with how they look. The percentage increased to 78% as the girls reached their teen years. Dianne Neumark Sztainer, the author of the book 'I'm, Like, SO Fat,' said that 30% of teen boys and 50% of teen girls go on diets and follow unhealthy eating patterns to lose weight easily. They vomit, skip meals, fast, use laxatives, and smoke cigarettes.

Body image is a significant factor affecting a person's self-esteem, and this issue is especially prevalent in women. Women are surrounded by unrealistic images of what they should look like. They are constantly told about the perfect body type they should have. The media objectifies women by making it seem like their bodies only exist for others and for the people around them to touch, look at, etc. The women depicted in music videos, movies, and on magazine covers differ greatly from the young girl going through puberty that looks at them and compares her body to theirs. This leads to feelings of inadequacy and unattractiveness.

Most women are affected by the way the media and people around them portray the idea of an ideal body. Young men are also not immune to this. Most young men have low self-esteem issues closely associated with body composition and weight, especially when it comes to muscle mass. It is unfortunate most people forget their body is not an object. Young men are often under a lot of pressure to build more muscle to show strength and masculinity.

When they do not live up to the expectations of society, they develop low self-esteem. They do everything in their power to emulate what they see. This only makes them feel worse about themselves.

Lack of Control

Most people feel overwhelmed in situations they cannot control. They find themselves getting swallowed in the world. This leaves them feeling powerless, ineffective, and worthless. Most people do not experience these emotions or feelings until they reach adulthood. Young people can go through existential crises where they question the meaning of their life. They wonder why they are in the world and why they matter. They lose control of themselves, and this makes them develop low self-esteem.

Unrealistic Goals

Most people tend to set unrealistic goals for themselves. You may set these goals for yourself because of the pressure that comes from within. If you expect too much of yourself, you will set unrealistic goals. Let us assume you are in school and have consistently been graded C in every course. You may set a goal for yourself to score A's in all your courses. It would make sense for you to set a goal to do better in one or more courses, but not all of them. This is an unrealistic goal since you cannot expect to improve in every course overnight. You should probably aim to achieve a B before you try to achieve an A.

Another mistake most people make is to want people around them to like them. This does not happen. Why do you think this is the case? You cannot expect everybody around you to like you no matter who you are. When you cannot meet unrealistic goals, you may feel like a failure in general.

Bad Choices in the Past

Have you ever thought about why you react to certain situations in the same way? This happens since you are locked in a specific pattern of reacting and decision-making. You may not have had good friends in the past. You probably did not go to the school of your choice. You may have had participated in different behaviors, such as unprotected sex or drug use. You do not do this simply because you are the person who behaves that way.

There is a possibility you may dislike yourself because of the choices you made in the past. You also believe you cannot change. It is for this reason you do not try. You continue to make these choices to reinforce the way you think about yourself.

NEGATIVE OR DESTRUCTIVE THOUGHT PATTERNS

When you think about yourself in a certain way, it becomes a habit.

You may have heard of the term muscle memory. When you repeatedly perform a specific type of activity, such as swimming or riding a bike, your brain sends a signal to your muscles to continue performing the activity to ensure you do not drown or fall off the seat. Your feelings, emotions, and thoughts also work this way. Your muscle memory can also learn the wrong way to perform different activities. Similarly, your thoughts, emotions, and feelings can learn inaccurate patterns.

If you find yourself having negative or destructive thoughts about yourself, especially your appearance, work, etc., you constantly think in the same way. You continue to feel this way until you take charge of your thoughts and emotions. You should challenge your thoughts and emotions to rewire your brain.

The causes mentioned above are not the only ones that lead to low self-esteem, but they are the most common causes. Most people have trouble with low self-esteem because of negative thought patterns. You may develop negative thought patterns because of multiple reasons. It is important for people to examine different situations in their lives, especially at school, work, social circle, etc. It is also important to examine their thoughts, emotions, and actions, especially when it comes to their bodies, a sense of purpose, past choices, and more. This method is the best way to examine the cause of low self-esteem.

CHAPTER SEVEN

TIPS TO OVERCOME LOW SELF-ESTEEM

If you suffer from low self-esteem, you do not believe you can change. Although, this is not true because you can become more confident when you change the way you think. This chapter has some tips to help you overcome low self-esteem and lead a happy life. It is important to understand low self-esteem is a learned behavior in some cases.

Improve Yourself

As mentioned in the previous chapter, various factors can cause low self-esteem. You cannot change what happened to you as a child, but there are some changes you can make to overcome low self-esteem.

For instance, if you have body image issues, you can make healthy changes to your diet and lifestyle. This helps you change your appearance and improves your self-esteem. If you are overweight, you can start an exercise routine or eat better to manage your weight.

You can make simple changes to your thoughts and actions to change the way you perceive yourself. For some people, this is the easiest way to overcome low self-esteem. If you are tired at all times and find this leads to low self-esteem, take a break after a few hours, so you get to sleep for at least 8 hours every night.

Here are some tips you can use to improve yourself.

Learn something new or upgrade an existing skill. Learning is the best idea for self-development. Thanks to technology, you can build your skills through online classes and communities. It could be learning a new language, learning to play a musical instrument or anything else you like. Just go out there, find what you want to learn, and master the lessons. You have it in you.

Start a business. If you have any little skill and oodles of self-believe, then starting a business is not an issue at all. Find what you are good at, and you can start a business as simple as teaching others your skills.

Work on your habits. If you have been in a codependent relationship for very long, you could have unwittingly given in to bad habits and forgotten the good ones you had earlier. Rediscover the old, good habits and bring them back into your life.

Were you a voracious reader before you got into this relationship? Were you a fitness freak? Did you practice singing and dancing regularly? Recover your lost personality. Remember, it is not irrevocably lost. It is lying somewhere deep within you. Delve into yourself and find it. And you will!

Accept Your Flaws

It is extremely easy to say this, but it is very hard for you to identify and accept your flaws. Having said that, if you want to improve your self-esteem, you should learn to accept everything about yourself. It is important to understand that everybody has some qualities they do not like. While many people around you may seem flawless, you never know how they feel about themselves. If you want to improve your self-esteem, focus only on your strengths, and see how you can use them to succeed in life. Do not concentrate only on your limitations.

Find a Hobby

One of the many characteristics of low self-esteem is the feeling of incompetence. If you have low self-esteem, you may think you are an underperformer and believe you cannot achieve anything in life. This, unfortunately, becomes a self-fulfilling prophecy.

If you want to improve your self-esteem, understand that you are capable of doing more in life. An easy way to do this is to pick a hobby or try a new activity. You can try something new, such as taking a pottery class or photography. Alternatively, you can try to do something daring, such as skydiving or parasailing. You can also try meditation since it helps you manage and control your thoughts.

Talk to Yourself

This may seem a little weird because who does that, right? But this process can help you overcome low self-esteem easily. Let us assume you are in a meeting and your boss is looking for new ideas to expand the business. You may have some brilliant ideas, but your low self-esteem makes you believe these ideas are not worthy. If you notice this happening, tell yourself that you are worthy and can speak your mind. Let your team know what your idea is. Since you cannot control how the people around you will take your idea, do not worry even if the team does not receive the idea well. Do not berate yourself for sharing it.

When it comes to overcoming low self-esteem, never let your negative thoughts or emotions change the way you act or behave. Learn to stand up to your thoughts and emotions and do what you believe is right for you. Your confidence will increase before you know it, and you will find yourself on the path to success.

Relax

One of the many things that contribute to low self-esteem is stress. When you are under too much stress, you begin to think negatively. You let these negative thoughts take charge and focus only on your weaknesses. This only increases your stress and lowers your self-esteem. Find an activity that relaxes you. Do things you love. Self-care should be your priority. Perform activities, such as meditation, gaming, taking a bath, dancing at home, and singing. These activities reduce stress and help you feel better.

Live in the Present

Another way to improve self-esteem is to focus only on the present and not on the past or future. It is best to live in the now. You can do this easily by engaging your senses. If you are in the park, find a calm place, and sit down. Close your eyes and listen to the sounds of nature. Feel the wind in your skin and smell the air. Your senses help you focus on the present. You can have the right frame of mind when you make decisions for yourself.

Be Kind

Does it make sense for you to be harsh to yourself but kind to the people around you? Isn't it also important for you to be kind to yourself? You can overcome low self-esteem when you treat yourself the way you would treat someone around you. Learn to be forgiving, kind, and gentle. You can use loving-kindness meditation to show yourself some love and kindness. Most people tend to kind to their family and friends, but they often forget to extend this kindness to themselves. When you accept yourself, you learn to love yourself, and this makes your self-esteem soar.

Know Your Strengths

It is important to identify your strengths to appreciate yourself. You need to understand that self-acceptance and self-appreciation are not the same things, but they are connected. If you do not accept yourself for who you are, you can never appreciate yourself.

To learn your strengths, you can sit down in a calm place with a piece of paper and pen. Take a deep breath. Begin to focus on various areas of your life and identify those areas where you think you can do better and then find a way to work on them.

People often set goals or targets they cannot accomplish. They tend to spend all their effort and time on tasks they cannot accomplish. It is important to know what your niche is and know what you are good at. When you know what your niche is, you can focus on working hard to achieve your goals. Everybody has areas they cannot excel at; so, do not criticize yourself if you fail at something.

Do Not Compare Yourself

Yes, there are many expectations about what your life should be like when it comes to society, your peers, and your family. You do not have to live up to these expectations. If you want to improve your self-esteem, you should learn to live on your terms and not try to please the people around you. Stop comparing your achievements with the people around you. Learn to set realistic goals. This will make it easy for you to follow your dreams. You must remember that every individual is different.

When you stop comparing yourself to the people around you, you will learn to be happier about whom you are.

Stop Negative Self-Talk

When you work on improving your self-esteem, it is important to remember that you are human. You, like everybody else, will make a mistake. Some people may make more mistakes when compared to others. One of the easiest ways to overcome low self-esteem is to stop beating yourself up when you make a mistake. This is the hardest thing to do, but you should learn to do this. It is a good idea for you to learn from your mistakes and store what you learn in your memory. You can then use this incident to keep you from making the same mistakes. Bear in mind that you learn from trial and error.

Surround Yourself with Positivity

As mentioned earlier, your thoughts, emotions, and feelings also use muscle memory. So, when you hear people constantly saying negative things about you, you tend to look at yourself negatively. This impacts your self-esteem. Some of these negative thoughts can have a permanent effect on your thoughts and emotions. The people you spend time with or interact with are indeed the ones who make you who you are today. If you want to feel better about yourself, you should never surround yourself with people who hate everything about you or just hate everything in general. Why should you befriend someone who does not have any ambition in life? Try to surround yourself with positive people. Attend conferences with those who want you to improve.

It takes a lot of patience and time to overcome low self-esteem. There will be times when you feel like you are only wasting your time since there is no way you can change. There will be some moments during your journey where you may choose to give up. You may also begin to associate yourself with the people around you who have no purpose in life. Never let these weak moments stop you from achieving your goals. Persevere and work hard to overcome these hardships and bumps. In the end, you will achieve all your goals and lead a successful and happy life.

CHAPTER EIGHT

UNDERSTANDING THE FEAR OF ABANDONMENT

The fear of abandonment stems from various developmental experiences, including some form of trauma or loss. It is a rather complicated fear and has been studied from various perspectives. There are several theories about why the fear of abandonment occurs in one's life. Some of the leading theories suggest it is due to any interruption in the regular or desirable development of cognitive and mental faculties in a human being. It includes any traumatizing or problematic life or social experiences and hardships faced in previous relationships. This is not classified officially as a phobia, but it is one of the most gripping and damaging fears one might harbor.

This fear can incline individuals to engage in thought patterns and behaviors that can harm their relationships. Ultimately, they end up with improper coping mechanisms to deal with this inherent fear. By doing this, they're unknowingly manifesting their fear of abandonment into reality. Yes, it becomes a self-fulfilling prophecy. The only way to tackle this fear is by thoroughly understanding it.

Understand the Reason

All the different things you learned in life and childhood fears affect your thoughts and behaviors. The person you are right now, including your thought patterns and behaviors, is a result of your childhood conditioning. Several theories try to explain why this fear occurs. Let us look at some of these theories.

Object Constancy

An individual's ability to maintain and cultivate relationships is based on one's early attachments with their primary caregivers, especially mothers or other maternal figures. The object-relations theory suggests that people or even certain physical items become a symbolic representation of a person or even a part of a person. When you put these two together, you end up with object relationships. This is a phrase that signifies the relationships we've all internalized in association with those people. This brings us to object constancy. It is a concept that suggests that even when we are not physically present with the other person, how we perceive them does not change. It is also associated with the concept of object permanence. Jean Piaget, a developmental psychologist, was among the first who studied the idea of object permanence. For instance, babies understand that objects will continue to exist even when they don't experience them directly.

Object constancy usually develops before the age of 3 years. As the child ages, he will grow and mature. The period of separation he experiences from his primary caregivers' increases. Maybe the child goes to school during weekdays, spends time with friends over the weekend, or goes away to boarding school. There are different reasons why the period of separation increases with age. A child with a positive object constancy knows that his important relationships are not damaged by the time that is spent apart.

Certain dramatic events, including death or separation of parents, can interrupt this object constancy. Even if the situation doesn't seem relevant or important to an adult, it affects the child's perception of relationships. This, in turn, will affect the role the relationship plays in his life. For instance, parents who barely spend time with their children or the ones who are neglectful increase the risk of interrupted object constancy in their children.

A Look at Mythology

Whether it is a rejected love or abandonment, mythology is filled with stories that include these components. In mythology, there are several instances where one person dedicated their entire being to their partners only to be left behind when the said person conquered the world. Carl Jung and other popular psychologists believe these stories from mythology and legends are embedded into our collective unconscious. Unknowingly, we have all internalized these myths and made them a part of how we perceive the world.

We also have certain personal myths that we don't share with others but reside within us. These personal myths are the manifestation of our interpretation of the collective unconscious while viewing it through our personal experiences. The fear of abandonment is associated with the universal myths we have all come to believe, and this is established through memories.

Previous Experiences

There are several significant life events we experience by the time we enter adulthood. It can be the death of a loved one, a bad breakup, the end of a friendship, or the transition from school to college, married life, and parenthood. There are several changes we experience. All these changes can leave you wondering where all the time went. Unknowingly, you start grieving for how life used to be before a tragedy occurred. If you experienced a traumatic or sudden abandonment, such as the loss of a loved one or the end of a long-term relationship, then fear of abandonment likely increases.

Signs to Watch Out For

Several people struggle with the fear of abandonment. Yes, you are not alone. There are different ways in which this fear manifests itself in one's life. If you are trying to determine whether you harbor this fear, here are some signs you should watch out for.

- You tend to attach yourself quickly to partners and relationships even if the other person isn't available.

- You have a tough time committing yourself fully to long-term relationships. Chances are you haven't had many long-term relationships.
- You have a constant need to please others because you seek their approval.
- You get stuck in unhealthy relationships because you are scared of moving on or ending it.
- You are a people pleaser and do this at your expense.
- You have a tough time expressing your emotions, and emotional intimacy scares you.
- You constantly engage in self-blame and are incredibly sensitive to criticism.
- You live with a feeling of general anxiety or depression.
- You often find yourself thinking thoughts laden with envy and jealousy whenever you meet others.
- You are insecure about who you are and believe you are not worthy of love.
- You believe others will leave you if they see who you are, and you are scared of showing your true self.
- You also experience severe anxiety when you are separated from the ones you love.
- There's a lot of repressed anger, frustration, and resentment within you.

If you have noticed any or all of these signs, chances are you have a fear of abandonment.

THE EFFECT OF THE FEAR OF ABANDONMENT

Fear of abandonment not only manifests itself in personal relationships but in other relationships too. Here is an example of how this fear tends to present itself in romantic relationships. The same cycle occurs in close friendships too.

The first phase of any relationship is the time spent getting to know one another. This is quite simple, and you probably feel safe at this stage. Since you are not emotionally invested in it, you continue to live your life as usual. After this, the honeymoon phase starts. This is the time when you decide to commit. You probably overlook all the red flags because you get along so well with the other person. You start spending a lot of time with the other person and enjoy it. It also makes you feel quite secure.

After this, the real relationship starts. This is when you are left to deal with the reality of the relationship. People get sick, money issues crop up, and there are arguments. It can be quite terrifying to navigate all this with a fear of abandonment. All these things that are normal aspects of a real relationship will seem frightening. They start thinking that their friend or partner is slowly pulling away from them and start missing the honeymoon phase.

The next aspect of the relationship is dealing with slights and the reactions. Since we are all humans, we are susceptible to mood swings and a difference in opinions. Regardless of how much you love and care for the other person, no one can spend all their time and effort focusing on a single individual. For an individual with the fear of abandonment, this might seem like a personal slight. For instance, an individual with this fear might start believing that their partner is withdrawing from the relationship because he or she doesn't reply to a text message immediately. This can become a turning point in any relationship. The perceived slight can make you believe that your partner no longer loves you. It results in unhealthy reactions that may only worsen the situation. You might become clingy, demanding, or even withdraw from the relationship. None of these things are desirable. When you become demanding and clingy, you are increasing the risk of codependency. If you start withdrawing, you will never form relationships.

COPE WITH THE FEAR OF ABANDONMENT

By learning new behavioral strategies and understanding your tendencies, you can overcome the fear of abandonment. If this fear is based on deep-rooted issues, you might need a little extra help. Asking for professional help is a good idea. It will help you work through your fears and change your thoughts and behaviors for the better. While coping with this fear, it is important to develop a sense of belonging. Instead of focusing all your time, energy, and resources on a single partner, concentrate on building healthier relationships in general. You need a group of close friends and loved ones. The only way to do this is by nurturing various relationships. Never put all your eggs in one basket. By building a community, your fear of abandonment will reduce.

Several people have this fear because they never had a sense of belonging growing up. Whatever is the reason, they probably felt incredibly disconnected from others. The good news is that you have complete control and power to change the situation. You are the only one that can do this. Surround yourself with individuals who genuinely care, love, and wish well for you. Find others you can share your interest with. Make a list of your dreams, hobbies, or passions. Once you have this list in place, look for others who share them. When you start networking and build healthy and stable relationships, you finally understand that you don't have to be scared of being abandoned. The ones who truly love and understand you will never abandon you. Don't expect this change to occur overnight. It takes time, a conscious effort, and plenty of patience.

CHAPTER NINE

UNDERSTANDING NEGATIVE SELF-TALK

People have an inner critic that voices opinions to protect them. At least, this is what people think. The inner critic makes it easy to stick to goals that work for you. Do you want to start a diet? This voice will help you do it. The voice will stop you if you want to try something new or different or something you tried before but failed. The voice uses all the memories in your subconscious mind. This means that the voice will use your past to determine the actions for your future. This does not benefit you in any way. The voice will harm you, especially if you are negative about life. The conversation you have with this voice is termed as negative self-talk, and it can bring you down even before you identify what happened to you.

There are different forms of negative self-talk, so you may have experienced this at some point in your life. If you are under stress because of this talk, your reactions and behavior will affect the people around you if you are not careful. This chapter sheds some light on what negative self-talk is and how it affects different aspects of your life.

INTRODUCTION TO NEGATIVE SELF-TALK

As mentioned earlier, negative self-talk has different forms. In some cases, it can keep you grounded. It will tell you what you need to do to stay safe and healthy. Other times it can sound mean by telling you that you can never do anything right. The voice also helps you determine the realistic approach you should take to achieve your goals. It may also develop a fear or fantasy.

The musings or thoughts of your inner critic can sound like a critical friend or partner from the past. This inner critic can take the path of cognitive distortions, such as catastrophizing and blaming, if you let it. In simple words, negative self-talk is the voice inside you that limits your abilities. It also prevents you from believing in your strengths, thereby making it difficult for you to achieve your dreams. These thoughts diminish your ability to change your life. Negative self-talk can be stressful, and it makes it harder for you to lead a happy and satisfying life.

FORMS OF NEGATIVE THINKING

Filtering

You tend to focus on the negative aspects of the situation and ignore the positive ones no matter what the situation is. Let us assume you have had a great presentation at work. The client loved the presentation and the ideas you pitched. You were able to finish work on time and leave. You will not look at these positive events because you think of the tasks you could not do or what someone said to you during the day. You only focus on the negative parts of your day.

Personalizing

It is important to remember that not every situation in life can be a happy one. When you find yourself in a bad situation, there is no point in blaming yourself. When you listen to your inner critic, you only focus on your contribution to the situation. For example, if your friends canceled on a night out, you assume nobody wanted to come because they do not like spending time with you.

Catastrophizing

You only look at the worst aspects of any situation. You also believe that everything will go wrong in your life. For example, if you stepped out of your house but walked into a neighbor who spilled coffee on your shirt, you will believe that everything in your day is going to be bad.

Polarizing

Situations or events will either be good or bad. There is nothing in the middle. You try to do everything perfectly so that there is no scope of anything going wrong. There will be times when the situation you are in will not work in your favor. You convince yourself that you are a failure.

EFFECTS OF NEGATIVE SELF-TALK

Negative self-talk can have terrible effects on you. Experts believe that people with low self-esteem and stress are often subjected to negative self-talk. This only makes it difficult to be happy in life. If you feel this way, you know that you cannot motivate yourself to do things differently. You should find a way to stop this self-talk from affecting every aspect of your life.

If you engage in negative self-talk frequently, you will be more stressed. This only happens because your reality is altered. You do not believe your success is something you can talk about. Negative self-talk makes it difficult for you to trust your strengths, and this makes it hard for you to capitalize on different opportunities. You perceive stress because of the change in behavior and perception. Some effects of negative self-talk are listed below.

Limited Thinking

Because of negative self-talk, you believe there is nothing you can do. If you tell yourself this frequently, you believe it. For example, if you tell yourself that you will not get a promotion because you are not worthy, you continue to believe that for the rest of your life.

Depressive Feelings and Emotions

I am sure you now understand that negative self-talk can make you feel depressed because you only have negative thoughts and emotions about yourself. Your inner voice can lead to significant damage if you do not check it early in life. For instance, telling yourself, you have no friends only leads to depression.

Perfectionism

Since negative self-talk only shows you the bad things about yourself, you try your best to hide those parts of yourself. You must be perfect, and that you can attain that level of perfection. High achievers usually perform better than perfectionists. Why do you think this happens? High achievers are happier and less stressed when they do a job well. They do not strive for perfection. Perfectionists often pick a task apart and see what they can do better next time.

Challenges in Relationships

If you listen to negative self-talk, you perceive yourself and the people around you differently. This voice can turn you into an insecure and needy person. You also tend to criticize the people around you because you are insecure about their achievements. It is because of this criticism that people will stay away from you.

Negative self-talk does not do anything good for you. Research shows that only positive thinking keeps you motivated to achieve your goals and succeed in life.

CHAPTER TEN

TIPS TO OVERCOME NEGATIVE SELF-TALK

Yes, it is true to have a realistic view of your strengths and weaknesses. This is the only way you can become a better person. Some criticism is always good for you since it helps to ground you. There is a difference between telling yourself that you are fat and telling yourself that you need to exercise more. More notably, your inner voice defines your successes and failures. It does this based on your past experiences. Unfortunately, your inner voice may criticize you excessively at times. This only backfires on your since you begin to focus only on your failures.

Let us assume you have made a mistake during work. Instead of focusing on what you could do to improve the situation, you worry about the consequences. As mentioned in the previous chapter, negative self-talk can lead to stress and depression. This chapter leaves you with some tips to overcome this negative self-talk.

Give Up the Negativity

When you beat yourself up for making a mistake, you give the mistake too much power. You may begin to look at yourself as a huge failure. If you continue to think negatively, you should take a few deep breaths. Now, divide the problem into small sections and try to identify a solution to the smaller sections before you look at the problem as a whole. Change the way you look at different situations in life, especially mistakes. For example, if you made a mistake on a test, do not tell yourself that you will fail the test. Calm down and focus on the positives. You only made one mistake and did everything else right. So, the chances of failure are low. The process becomes easier if you look only at the positives and ignore the negatives. This helps you determine what box the problem fits in, which helps you develop the confidence you need to succeed.

I know it is easier said than done. You cannot always think positively about everything in life, especially if you are upset. Experts say that it only makes the situation worse when you say positive things to yourself when you are upset. Your brain refuses to believe this because it perceives them as lies. They suggest you use a method known as possible thinking. In this method, you focus only on neutral thoughts to change the way you perceive the situation. For example, if you just finished writing a test, instead of telling yourself you will fail, tell yourself, "I think I did well enough to be graded a B." It becomes easy to identify the path to take when you look at the facts and choose objectively.

Trust Yourself

Let us assume you were in a meeting, and when the boss called upon you, you said the first thing on your mind. You may have been thinking about your plants and whether you watered them this morning and made a statement about it. Yes, you may have made a fool of yourself, but if you look at the situation, you see that nobody in the room was paying attention. Everybody was either typing into their laptop or looking at the presentation. Don't be harsh on yourself.

If you look at a situation objectively, you stop worrying about what someone may say about you. For example, instead of telling yourself for being stupid to say that in front of everybody, tell yourself you made a mistake and move on. Here are some more tips to help you build self-trust.

Be yourself – Do not try to be anyone else but yourself because you are born to be YOU, a unique and beautiful person. Do not try to change yourself for others because an inauthentic personality is neither good for you nor for the people who love you. The only way you can be your best self is by being authentic and living your true personality.

Spend time with yourself – The first step to be yourself is to know yourself. And for this, you must spend time with yourself. This time is to get acquainted with your strengths and weaknesses, likes and dislikes, and your desires and dreams. When you know yourself, you understand yourself better, which, in turn, helps you to trust yourself better.

Set reasonable goals for yourself – For example, if you are planning on starting a business, don't expect to make large amounts of money in your first attempt. Start small and take baby steps towards your final goal by working on little milestones right through the journey. The success you see at each baby step will help you build self-trust.

Choose a Positive Outlook

You must change the way you look at different situations. Do not tell yourself you cannot achieve anything in life. If you have a busy day ahead of you, do not demotivate yourself by saying you cannot complete your tasks. Instead, sit down and list down the tasks. Prioritize and meet your goals.

This may seem silly, but a change in how you look at things gives you the impression that you can achieve anything. You also learn that a moment is just a moment. When you tell yourself you are stupid, you are defining who you are. When you say you felt stupid, you know you are not stupid, and the situation made you feel that way.

Be Kind to Yourself

You are bound to make mistakes in life and at work. When you make this mistake, you will tell your friend about how bad you felt after making a mistake. How does your friend react when you make this mistake? Is he kind to you? Or does he call you stupid and walk away? Another thing to remember is that you should always speak to yourself the way your friend speaks to you. You know your friend will never call you a slob, so why should you call yourself one?

Give the Critic a Name

If you want to make things a little light, refer to your inner critic using a funny name. Do you think you can take it seriously if you give it a funny name? Let us assume you call your inner critic the Grinch. Do you think you can pay attention to what it has to say to you if you call it that? No. Right? Why do you think this is the case? When they give the inner critic funny names, you can break free from the hold it has over you. This gives you the strength to break free from anxiety.

Some psychologists also say you should give some of your inner thoughts, names. Name every thought that passes through your mind and every memory you have ever made. If you step back and listen to the stories, you realize the premise of most stories is the same. The same thoughts pass through your mind regularly, and when you name them, you learn to ignore them.

Talk to Someone

Do not have too many secrets. This only makes you feel bad about yourself. For example, if you go to a party and do something silly, instead of worrying about how people perceive you, leave the place and call your friend. When you tell him the things you did at the party, he will laugh. When this happens, you no longer feel any shame. It is best to find the right person to speak to, so you can laugh and get over something without obsessing over it.

Accept Yourself

Stop holding yourself to high standards. Set realistic goals and expectations. It is destructive to be a perfectionist. No successful leader will tell you they believe they are perfect. You cannot expect anybody to be perfect. The idea of perfectionism is a lie. Successful people credit their success to mistakes they make and eventually learn from them. They talk about how it formed their character and made them reach their goal. Ease your principles a little and be empathetic towards yourself. These steps will make it easy for you to overcome your negative self-talk.

CHAPTER ELEVEN

EXERCISES TO REMOVE NEGATIVE SELF-TALK

It is important to remember that every thought you have shapes your reality. If you only have negative thoughts, you will look at life negatively. Every thought, emotion, or feeling you have is based on the memories stored in your subconscious mind. When you are aware and in control of what is happening in your mind, you can change your innate beliefs and thoughts. When you change these thoughts, you can change who you are.

In the previous chapters, we looked at what negative self-talk is and also some tips you can use to silence your inner voice. This chapter has some exercises you can use to overcome negative thoughts and change the way you think. When you notice yourself thinking negatively, you can use these exercises to change your thoughts.

If you lead a busy schedule, you cannot practice these exercises every day, so set a reminder for yourself. Set aside some time every morning or night to perform these exercises.

Track your progress using either sticky notes or journals. You can use these sticky notes to remind you about the activities. Stick these notes in your bathroom, bedroom, kitchen, and every other place in your house that you frequently visit to remind you that it is time to perform the exercise. You may not need constant reminders, but if you want to change the way you speak to yourself you need to do this. Let us look at some exercises that you can regularly perform to change the way you think.

Positive Affirmations

Positive affirmations are the best way to change the way you think. You can choose different positive affirmations to help you change the way you think based on your wants and needs. You can repeat these affirmations to yourself throughout the day. When you use positive affirmations, you can change all your negative thoughts into positivity. This means you should check your thoughts. If you identify that you are thinking negatively, you can use a positive affirmation to change the way you think. This will help you change the way the negative thought makes you feel. Using positive affirmations, you can identify the beliefs that make you think negatively. You can remove and replace negative thoughts through positive affirmations and beliefs. Affirmations work since they work on the principles of the law of attraction. It is important to understand that you attract everything you believe. Some positive

affirmations are given below to help you get started:

I give up all my old habits and ready to embrace new, positive ones.

I let go of my critical inner voice and choose to trust myself.

I can see the challenges and obstacles clearing up on my success journey.

I embrace learning and self-improvement.

I control my life and emotions.

I am filled with positivity.

I start afresh today on a clean slate, ready to write the good things of my life.

I am positive and awesome.

Good Memories

It is important to note that you will never be in the same place in your life. Where you are today is completely different from where you were yesterday. Change is constant in life. You may deny this, but there is always some big or small change that has happened in your life. You may be better at a task, or things may have taken a turn for the worse. You may not be moving in the direction you want to, and this area of your life may have been better before. Things may not have been great then, but that would not have bothered you. When you are in these situations tell yourself about an event that happened in the past where things were alright. This will help you control the negative emotions you may have about the current situation.

Your friends may remind you about the better times in life. Facebook, Instagram, and other social media platforms may remind you about a good memory from your past. You should learn to cherish these memories. Make sure you do not become the person you were a few years ago. All you must do is realize that this moment is precious, and it will be a memory in the distant future. No matter how you feel about the situation, take some time to talk to yourself. Understand the moment in your past that left an impression on you. This memory will change your mindset. There is an interesting way to get habituated to recalling a good memory. Use these pointers.

Find a quiet, undisturbed spot. Close your eyes and take a couple of deep breaths. Make sure you are relaxed completely.

Now, recall a pleasant memory that you want to embed in your conscious mind. It could be anything, a beautiful place you visited, a wonderful experience you had, the face of someone who loves unconditionally, or anything else that makes you happy.

As you recall the memory, bring the tips of your thumb and forefinger together so that they touch each other. This is the physical connection to your memory. You have related this particular gesture to the happy memory. Keep doing this exercise every day for about 3 weeks.

You will notice something interesting after a while. Every time you do this simple exercise, your mind will recall that happy memory. So, the next time you feel sad, and your inner critical voice tries to get the better of you, make this gesture, and the happy memory will wipe out your current negativity.

You can have separate gestures for various good memories and recall them as and when you wish. This method is literally like having good memories at your fingertips.

Short Stories

Write down short stories to keep you positive and happy. You can write about your past or some memory you always want to cherish. Use this method when you feel like you are having a bad day or when you are upset or low. You can use this technique in two ways:

If you find yourself thinking negatively about a situation, reel your thoughts back in. Instead of using positive affirmations, tell yourself a story of how the future can look for you. Instead, tell yourself a story. Tell yourself about your hopes and dreams. When you do this, you stop worrying yourself with negativity and create a healthy and positive space for yourself. You learn to expect that only good things will happen.

This method is like the first, except that you will tell yourself a story that is not related to the negative thought. You cannot expect to always think positively because it is not good for the mind. When you find yourself thinking negatively, use the story to replace your thoughts. The story can be about an unrelated topic. To do this, you should tell yourself a story of your possible future that is related to any other aspect of your life.

Ho'oponopono Process

The Ho'oponopono Process is an ancient Hawaiian healing process. It uses your energy to change the way you act and think. This exercise has helped many people remove negative thoughts and foster positive thinking. Using this exercise, you only alter the way you think or feel. This change also makes it easier for you to change your body. This is because the process works only on your energy and uses that energy to heal you.

Ho'oponopono is a Hawaiian word that means "to make doubly right" or to make it right for ourselves, as well as with others around us. This ancient technique is a loving and positive way of forgetting old connections and renewing them in new ways. The forgetting process involves forgiving mistakes as well as getting rid of biases that have been built up over the years.

This healing technique can help you overcome your negative thoughts by cutting off your connection with them for a while and renewing the connection by looking at them in a new, positive light. It might make sense to speak to a facilitator in your area (or try reaching out to someone through the internet) and learn the ways of this technique.

CHAPTER TWELVE

POSITIVE THINKING

Have you ever wondered what positive thinking is? Or how you can determine if you think positively? I am sure you were asked this question numerous times – is the glass in front of you half empty or half full? The answer to this question helps you determine your attitude towards your life and yourself. The answer to the question also changes the way you think.

Traits like pessimism and optimism change the way you think and look at different situations in life. If you are an optimist, you always look at the positive aspects of any situation. This means you have a positive approach towards any situation that makes it easier for you to manage your stress. This improves your mental wellbeing. If you are pessimistic, you will focus only on your negative self-talk. Do not worry since you can change the way you think easily.

When I say positive thinking, I do not mean you should forget about unpleasant situations. I only mean that you should focus on the positives, even in unpleasant situations. If you think positively, you can overcome any unpleasant situation constructively and effectively. You stop believing that every situation in your life is bad.

You can only start thinking positively if you stop negative self-talk. You can change the stream of negativity into positivity using the steps mentioned in the previous chapter. As mentioned earlier, your inner critic uses the memories and information stored in the subconscious mind. The advice the voice gives you may arise from different misconceptions you create.

BENEFITS OF POSITIVE THINKING

Research is still underway to understand the different effects of positive thinking on your mind and body. Some of these benefits are:

- Lower levels of depression
- Increased life span
- Resistance to diseases like the common cold
- Lower levels of distress
- Better physical and psychological well-being
- Reduced risk of cardiovascular diseases
- Better heart health
- Healthy coping mechanisms during times of hardship and stress

Further research is needed to understand how positive thinking improves mental and physical health. There is a theory that positive thinking can help you overcome stressful situations. This reduces the effects that stress has on your body. If you have a positive approach to life, you can lead a healthier life since you know what is good for your body and what is not.

TIPS FOR PRACTICING POSITIVE THINKING

It is easy to turn your negative thoughts into positive ones, and we have looked at some tips in the previous chapter. The process is easy, but it will take a lot of patience, practice, and time. Since you are developing a new habit, you need to practice as often as you can. This section gives you some tips that you can use to start thinking positively.

Find the Areas to Change

If you want to think positively, you should sit down and focus on the aspects of your life you want to make a change to. These aspects can include everything in your life, such as relationships, work, education, or travel. It is easier to start small. Choose one area in your life you want to change and focus on that area. You can look at the situation in different ways and find a way to improve it.

Evaluate Your Thoughts

You must take some time every day to pause and evaluate your thoughts. If your thoughts are negative, you should find a way to change them to positive thoughts.

Laugh More

If you find yourself in a difficult situation, you should try to laugh it off or change your thoughts. Look for the humor in a situation. Experts believe that laughing off a bad situation will make you feel better and provide a way for you to take care of the situation with renewed energy. Here are some ways you can increase laughter in your life:

Set the intent to laugh more often in your life. Repeat the affirmation every morning when you wake up, "I will laugh a lot today."

Find a way to include something funny in your morning routine. For example, read your favorite cartoon every morning while you eat breakfast or any other convenient time. Or watch a short, funny video. Anything that makes you laugh in the morning is a great way to start a day.

Smile a lot too. Although smiling and laughing may seem different, the benefits are more or less the same. Find reasons to smile more every day. Smile to yourself without reason as well. The more you habituate yourself to smiling and laughing, the more positivity will enter your life.

Make friends with witty people - Interact with funny and happy people. People who can make you laugh are the best kind of people to have in your life to balance off the negativity.

Follow a Healthy Lifestyle

Keep yourself active. Make sure to exercise for at least 30 minutes on four or five days of the week. You can increase or decrease the time you spend on exercise, depending on how active you are. It is important to exercise since that releases the dopamine hormone that keeps you happy throughout the day. Try sticking to a healthy diet.

Surround Yourself with Positivity

Make sure the people around you are positive and that you can depend on them when you find yourself under immense stress. Try to stick to a group of friends who are willing to give you the necessary advice. They also should be brave enough to give you constructive feedback. People who are negative only increase your stress levels and make you doubt your abilities.

If you have looked at life negatively, you cannot expect to change the way you think or feel overnight. It is only with practice that you can change the way your inner voice thinks. You learn to accept yourself for who you are and will accept everything that life throws at you with renewed energy and enthusiasm. If you are optimistic, you can constructively handle stress, and this ability you must develop.

CHAPTER THIRTEEN

UNDERSTANDING THE INFERIORITY COMPLEX

You may feel inferior at different points in your life. If you have had negative events in life, you may feel inferior to different people, including a sibling, friend, or peer. For some, it can be the start of a major inferiority complex even though it may have been just a minor event for others. Most people develop this complex during their childhood, and the complex will manifest itself into various aspects of your life. If you do not recognize these symptoms early on in life, you will suffer in the future. You may belittle yourself and become very sensitive.

People with such limitations need to determine, accept, and overcome their limitations when they reach a certain age in life. Some people constantly remember their limitations because of an authoritative adult, parent, or friend. They may also succumb to peer pressure because of these limitations. These limitations include cultural differences, disabilities, emotional responses, and physical appearances. These people exhibit some inferiority complex symptoms because of these reminders. They develop some defense mechanisms to overcome these feelings. They use these mechanisms when someone around them speaks to them about their insecurities.

How is Inferiority Complex and Feeling Inferior Different?

The only time you should have felt inferior was when you were a baby. You were dependent on your parents and could never survive on your own. As you grow up, you become stronger and develop skills that make you more capable of handling the different situations life throws you in.

Alfred Adler, a famous psychologist, mentioned that it is a healthy motivation to feel inferior. When you see someone perform better than you or receive constructive criticism, you will do whatever you can to improve, so you are as good as him or her. It is only when you do this that you motivate yourself to change. You want to feel powerful. According to you, this is the only way you can stop feeling inferior. When you feel inferior, you take some time to learn more from the people who make you feel this way. You work towards developing yourself and will eventually become a confident adult.

For some people, the feeling of inferiority may be overwhelming. This feeling of inferiority is the inferiority complex. This complex paralyzes you. You cannot perform any activity you were good at, which results in social anxiety or shyness. You may also begin to feel worthless, and your fear of failure will make it difficult for you to do anything in life.

This is the difference between feeling inferior and the inferiority complex. If you feel inferior, you can change the way you think. You can also change how you look at life. If you have an inferiority complex, it means you feel unworthy and incomplete. You cannot work on any task you are good at performing. You also find it difficult to visualize that you will achieve something in the future.

TYPES OF INFERIORITY

Most people follow a specific pattern when it comes to their inferiority complex. Based on these patterns, people with inferiority complex fall into two categories:

- Even though some people know they are successful, smart, and good-looking they feel inferior to their peers and friends. This is a mysterious feeling. They never know why they feel they are not good enough. If you feel this way and let people know about how you feel. Unfortunately, you do not know why you feel this way either. It is an innate feeling.
- Some people know they are not as good as the people around them. They are boring, failure, dumb, etc. Such people only focus on their flaws that make it difficult for them to understand people and how they are trying to support them. If you fall into this category, you think you can only solve a problem or improve your life if you were smart, good-looking, and successful. You may give yourself any other reason to feel this way. Here is a quick test - how would you complete the following

sentence: "I will be confident, attractive and happy, if only I was ______________________________."

Are you sure of the category you fall into? People who fall under the first category cannot believe they are good at what they do. Those in the second category believe they behave the way they do because they only focus on the flaws. No matter which category you fall in, it is possible you were stuck with this feeling for most of your life.

CHAPTER FOURTEEN

SIGNS OF INFERIORITY COMPLEX

This chapter lists some signs to help you determine if you have an inferiority complex.

Being Overly Sensitive

When you have an inferiority complex or feel inferior, any comment about you or your work will only leave you feeling depressed. You may hate yourself for days or weeks because of what someone said about you. You feel miserable when someone rejects you or excludes you from any conversation. You do your best to try to stop caring for what others say about you, but it is not simple for you to do this.

You may have read numerous articles and books to determine how you can handle these comments. Most of these articles and books tell you not to worry about what people around you have to say about you. They tell you to consider a rational argument to help you stop thinking negatively about yourself. You may have come across multiple articles that tell you that another person's opinion about you does not matter. It is easier said than done. This advice does not help since most people have difficulty in reasoning with their emotions.

Caring less for another's opinion is the only way to stop feeling this way. You should only worry about how you perceive yourself. People who do not care about what someone has to say about them only trust their values.

If your sense of judgment is strong and your morals and beliefs are strong, you stop worrying about how someone thinks about you. This is an important thing to do, and it will take time for you to find your beliefs and stick to them. Some people may tell you that you know who you are. You may not have known what that meant. It is important to note that a person who has deep-rooted beliefs and values is attractive. If you have strong beliefs, it means you are not a pushover.

Constantly Comparing Your Qualities

When you compare your abilities and characteristics with the people around you, you either feel superior or inferior to them. Let us look at the problem a little closer. Why do you believe that everybody is always more successful and better when compared to you? You only do this because you focus on the other person's best qualities and use those qualities to compare yourself.

It is important to remember that people who are good at one thing may not be better at others. You may have some qualities that the other person wants. For instance, if someone spends at least an hour at the gym, he or she is going to have a better body than you. If a classmate of yours succeeds academically every semester, it is because he or she works hard and prepares for the exam well. If you look at these people, you tell yourself that you are worse than them because you cannot do what they can do. You begin to feel inferior. Yes, indeed, you are not going to be as good as they are. Since you measure your qualities and success against changing criteria, you tend to feel inferior. You should remember that you could only be successful if you work hard in that area. This means the people you compare yourself to may neglect other areas in their life. Make sure you settle for the best version of yourself. This will relieve you of your need to always meet another's standards. You must remember to stop comparing yourself with the people around you.

Submissive Behavior

Have you heard of the theory called social rank in psychology? According to this theory, a person's perceived social status or rank directly determines how their behavior. If you feel inferior or superior to someone, you believe your status is different from theirs and tend to act accordingly. Many traits a person develops are because of how they perceive themselves. Think of how shy people often act:

- Can never make eye contact
- Always talk softly
- Are afraid to assert their opinions

Let us assume a monkey were to act this way. How would a scientist explain this behavior? He would say the monkey is displaying submissive behavior. It is from here that low confidence stems. A submissive person behaves the way he does because of a subconscious belief. He believes people around him are superior, better, and deserve more respect when compared to them. If you can overcome this feeling of insecurity, you will find it easier to be outgoing.

Perfectionism

Both inferiority and perfectionism are complementary since the roots for both are in comparison. If you are a perfectionist, you will never be happy with what you do. Consider the following scenario:

Emily had always wanted to be an artist, and she did everything she could to improve. Unfortunately, she is a perfectionist and believed that this characteristic of hers would help her become the best artist there is. This is not what happened, though. Emily visited online galleries and learned more about others' art from those galleries. She did her best to learn different forms of art to help her improve. When she looked at others' paintings, she was never happy because she thought the other artists painted better than she did. She did not think her work could ever match up to what the others did and stopped painting. According to her, none of the famous artists in those galleries would appreciate her work. Her comparison and need for perfection became unhealthy, and she soon began to feel inferior to her competitors. She stopped painting because of this feeling of inferiority. She did not pick up a brush for years because she knew she could never meet her expectations.

When you strive to be perfect, you do not focus on the quality of work. This means the result is not as good as it could have been. Some people are born with the abilities that help them be the people they are. Most people do not excel in their field because they put too much pressure on themselves. Malcolm Gladwell said it takes a person at least 10,000 hours to reach a certain level of greatness or genius in an industry. The artists Emily admired were in their late 50s, so they had enough time to improve their skills.

TRIGGERS OF JEALOUSY, GUILT, OR SHAME

Social media is both a blessing and a curse. When you look at people's Instagram handles or Facebook pages, you begin to compare your life to theirs. This only makes you feel inferior. You begin to doubt yourself. For example:

- You see that your friends at college are out partying and are socializing, while you stay at home.
- Your friends have many likes on their posts, but that makes you feel worthless or insignificant since you do not receive those many likes for your posts.
- You see that all your friends are starting their families. This makes you question if you are making the right decisions.

It is important to remember that people always use social media to present the perfect parts of their lives. You never know what they are going through, and when you compare your life to theirs, you are only looking at one aspect of their life. Social media often makes people feel bad about their lives, and the problem worsens if they have an inferiority complex.

Judging Others

Let us consider some situations or patterns you may have noticed by now. Let us assume you have a friend who has always been rejected by women for being different. He will soon hate them. If you have an unmarried friend, you see them act bitter and horrible if they are in a room with a happy couple. They do this because the people around them remind them about their inferior feelings and emotions. They worry about their insecurities, fears, looks, and failure.

When a woman looks at newspapers or magazine covers and finds a skinny supermodel on the cover, she will worry about the unrealistic standards that society has. She is not trying to understand what makes her mad. When she looks at the picture of the supermodel, she compares her body to the model's body, which triggers feelings of unworthiness and unattractiveness inside her. She may feel that she is not as valuable as the supermodel and not as attractive as she is. She then begins to believe that the people around her also perceive her in the same way. Women believe their value is solely dependent on their appearance. Unlike women, men do not always compare their appearances, and nobody knows why. However, some men worry about how people perceive them since most men are expected to have muscle mass and lean bodies. Many activists have started to petition against the images in magazines and newspapers. Do you know what I am trying to say now? Let us look at another example.

You may notice some friends making fun of rich people or millionaires for wearing expensive suits or driving an expensive car. Why do you think they do this? They want to cover their feeling of inadequacy since they cannot afford expensive suits. If they were to win a lottery, they would buy themselves an expensive car or suit.

You need to understand that your inferiority makes you judge people around you. When you judge someone, you try to make yourself feel better. This method backfires since you become spiteful. Start identifying the moments when you condemn other people and feel hateful. When you do this, you identify the things about yourself you do not like. It is important to remember that what you say about the people around you merely reflect the emotions and feelings within you. If you do not judge people often, you will not constantly feel judged.

Hiding Flaws without Success

Most people who are insecure try to hide the parts of themselves they do not like. For instance, if you think you are ugly, you will not do anything to change the way you feel. You only hide what you are ashamed of.

- Strike the same pose in a photograph.
- You wear baggy clothing to avoid looking at your body shape.

- If you have crooked teeth, you may stop smiling. You may want to hide your teeth. If you have braces, you cover your mouth whenever you talk.
- You may wear makeup or hide your face if you do not want people to look at your acne.

This means you worry about how people see you. You want to control how they perceive you, and you do everything in your power to stop letting them identify things you do not like about yourself. You only feel stressed out and self-conscious from the constant need to stay alert.

CHAPTER FIFTEEN

HOW TO STOP BEING INFERIOR

If you feel inferior to your peers, friends, and family, use the tips mentioned in this chapter to help you change the way you perceive yourself. When you work on these tips, focus on yourself, and practice every day to change your life. Implement the strategies mentioned in the book immediately.

Look at Your Circle

If you want to change things about your life, you need to focus on your life and identify the parts working for you and those that are not. If you are doing great in your career, but do not have any confidence in your relationship, find a way to change the way you feel about your relationship. If you think you need professional help to improve your relationship, then take that step. Learn to communicate better or listen better. You decide to change the parts of your life that do not work for you.

Replace the Negativity

You may be overweight, clumsy, uneducated, or shy. This does not mean you are not intelligent. Learn to be kind to yourself. Make a list of the reasons you put yourself down. Find a positive way to say it. Remove the negativity by changing the way you tell things. If you are clumsy, stop calling yourself that. Instead, tell yourself you should learn to walk gracefully. Identify the characteristics and traits that you feel bring you down. Identify the people around you that make you feel inferior. There are people around you who will find a way to put you down. They may do this because of how they feel about themselves. So, forgive them and remove them from your life. Is it your co-worker, a successful person, or your partner? How do these people make you feel bad about yourself? Is there a new skill you can develop that will help you to feel better about yourself?

Do Not Try to Be Someone Else

It is great to have a role model. You may want to succeed or grow in life like your role model. You can learn from them. The one thing you should do is to avoid acting like them because you lose your individuality. Do not expect to be someone you are not. You should, instead, focus on the characteristics of the people around you who you admire. You should try to emulate those characteristics. Make sure to keep your individuality.

Some more simple tips to be yourself and eliminate the desire to be someone else:

Don't focus on pleasing others - If you focus on doing everything to please others, you lose touch with your core self. Avoid this. Always do things that make you happy first.

Don't worry excessively about other people's opinions - Sometimes, it is good to listen to the advice of your well-wishers for self-improvement, but if you make it your sole purpose to live according to others' whims and fancies, you will always feel uncertain of yourself, and your confidence levels will always be low. Therefore, don't worry excessively about others' opinions and learn to trust your needs and intuition.

Identify the Cause

Most people believe a weakness or flaw in them is the reason for every problem in life, but this is not true. It is important to stop believing that. It is important to remember that these flaws are a part of you. They make you who you are. There is no simple solution to help you change the situation. Identify the root cause of the problem before you try to solve it.

Focus on Success

It is important to focus on your successes, small or big. Most leaders practice this regularly to help them succeed in any venture. Everybody fails, and this is something you should accept. As someone once said, 'Failures are the steppingstone to success.' If you want to improve, learn from your mistakes, and change the way you think about failures.

People go through their day with the impression that every person around them knows what their flaws are. They fear that people around them will not like them because of those flaws. This, however, is not true since nobody knows someone that well. Sure, you may be clumsy, but they may not pay attention to that since they are busy in their world. They may not have had the time to consider your flaws. The truth is that most people around you are not thinking about you. Next time you are at a family gathering pay attention to the conversations if you think this is untrue. Most people complain about how terrible their life is. They do not talk about your clumsiness, your body type, or anything else, so remember you are free.

Know What You Like About Yourself

You may develop an inferiority complex because of the people around you. People always compare you to people they know, and this comparison makes you wonder why the other person is better than you. You should stop letting these comparisons get to you. You should change how you perceive yourself. Let us assume you are short. Why does being short make, you feel inferior? Is it because it's a flaw? Visualize what it would be like if you were taller. Does that make you a happier person? Is it something you can relate to? Do you feel like yourself? Do you think you can become taller now? Use this method to understand or imagine how you would feel in different situations.

Ask a Friend to Tell You What They Like about You

It is easier to ask someone you trust to list his or her favorite things about you. You know what they are, but you do not trust yourself. It feels great when someone lists your qualities. You learn to be more confident. There are times when you do not know who you are. But, if a friend tells you what the best part about you, then you will feel better about yourself. If you want them to elaborate, ask them to do so. You may want to know why they think that you have a specific quality. Ask them to give you examples.

CHAPTER SIXTEEN

TIPS TO CONTROL YOUR MIND

As mentioned earlier, your negative thought patterns, feelings, and emotions are a learned process. I am sure you know that the brain controls everything that happens in your body, that is, both the voluntary and involuntary reactions. There are two parts to your brain - the conscious and subconscious. Your reactions, emotions, and thoughts are based on all the memory stored in your subconscious mind. You need to break free of your subconscious mind to confirm you do not behave based on an event that occurred in the past.

You might have the physical ability, talent, and/or skills to do something. When you think you cannot do it, you will find a reason why you cannot do it. This is a common problem that people face when they have low self-esteem and self-worth. For example, if you were to pitch an idea to your boss, you may not do it since your mind believes your ideas cannot impress anybody. You believe this, too, but the idea you have may help the company improve. You need to speak up. The only way you can change the way you think is by controlling your mind.

Well, given that all your reactions and emotions spring forth from your mental processes, it is only logical for you to control these processes. In simple words, you should "conquer your mind." This chapter has some tips to help you do the same.

IDENTIFY AND RE-PROGRAM YOUR TRIGGERS

Most thoughts and emotions arise when there is a trigger, and some of these triggers make you develop low self-esteem. For instance, if someone told you since you were a child, you will not amount to anything in life, you will continue to believe that as you grow up. So, if someone tells you now that you cannot do much or your idea is terrible, you will take it to heart. Your subconscious mind will remember all the memories in the past where someone told you this and will hold you back from achieving your dreams. You cannot let this happen. Think of your mind like a program. The output of a program changes depending on the type of data you feed it. This means you can change the memories or alter the triggers to ensure that your mind does not focus on those aspects that only give you pain and sorrow. It is difficult to re-program your mind. You will feel uncomfortable, but you cannot overcome something if you stay in your comfort zone. You have to step out of it.

You can condition your mind to respond to different situations. Do not let your mind rely only on your subconscious to respond to a situation. Change the way you act and think. Think about people who wear contact lenses. Do you think their eyes like it when a foreign object is placed in them? No. They had to overcome the reflex.

One way to change your response is by thinking things through. When you tell yourself, you cannot do something because you are worthless, stop, and rethink the situation. Is the reason for your refusal valid? How so? Is it valid, or are you justifying it? When you think things through more you will realize that there is no reason to control your progress.

If you are unsure of your triggers, sit down in a calm place with a pen and paper. Close your eyes and focus on the different memories or situations in life that led you to behave the way you do. Once you identify these triggers, decipher the responses and see how you can change them. It will be uncomfortable for you to do this, but with practice, it will become easier.

Do Not Focus Too Much on Yourself

If one focuses too much on self, it can lead to one of the reasons they do not like themselves. They worry about how people perceive them. If you think along the same lines, stop yourself now. If you worry too much about what someone around you has to say about you, you can never excel in life. You cannot achieve your goals or dreams. The result is that you keep yourself from doing certain things because you are afraid to be embarrassed.

If you want to get rid of this habit, turn your attention to other people. If your attention is placed elsewhere, you stop worrying about how people perceive you. This does not mean you should judge the people around you.

Visualize Success

One of the main reasons you may have low self-esteem is because you think you are a failure. This fear prevents you from trying anything new. So, it helps if you think differently. Condition yourself into thinking you will succeed. Close your eyes and visualize success. This is one way to convince yourself that success is not too far away from you. Imagine yourself in a situation where you think you cannot succeed. Focus on how you will feel when you achieve your goals. Repeat this process every day and visualize a different situation every time. It is best to do this when you start your day since that helps you change the way you feel throughout the day. Involve as many of your senses as possible when you perform this exercise to make the visualization real.

Carry Yourself Confidently

Another way to control your mind is to maintain proper posture. When you stand tall, the people around you will perceive you as a confident individual. As a result, you also feel that way about yourself. When you feel this way about yourself, you will act that way as well. Research shows that proper posture has numerous benefits, and people who have proper posture are confident. Some body postures that project confidence in your personality are given below for your use:

Maintain an assertive posture - When you stand, your legs and shoulders must be aligned with each other. Make sure your feet are about 4-5 inches apart while ensuring your body weight is equally distributed on both your feet. Imagine a string pulling your head from above, which will help you stand erect. Your stance will exude confidence.

Use power poses - Amy Cuddy, an American social psychologist, talks highly of power poses that build confidence and inner strength. One particularly popular power pose the professor-cum-TED talk expert talks about is the Wonder Woman pose. You stand with your hands on your hips and legs a foot apart and breathe in before you make an entry into a meeting. You can use this pose before a difficult conversation with your partner, mother, child, or anyone else with whom you have a codependent relationship. You will find it easier to express your opinions and needs better, and you will look and feel confident.

Listen

When you have low self-esteem, it becomes hard for you to speak up to the people around you. Since you have zero confidence in your abilities, you avoid voicing your opinion. If you have to say something, you probably mumble something unintelligible and walk away. The person you are talking to cannot understand what you are saying, so you have to repeat yourself. If you do not want to repeat what you said, you may want to run away. A good way to prevent these situations is to listen to what you think about yourself.

Listening to yourself and your thoughts will help you find the right words to express them out to the people around you. Avoid saying things impulsively to prevent coming to say something you don't really mean or want to say. Listen to your needs first and then articulate them clearly, confidently, and fearlessly.

Do Not Compare

I have been saying this repeatedly, and I will say it again - "You are unique." This may be a cliché, but it is true. Why is it important for you to understand this? Well, one reason you lack confidence and have low self-esteem is that you compare yourself to the people around you. Feeling inadequate because of comparisons with others intimidates you. Avoid comparisons if you can. If you find yourself doing this, remember to be objective and realistic. You must understand that you are different. You do not have to measure up to a friend or neighbor. The only thing you need to focus on is improving yourself.

Identify Your Strengths

You need to focus on your achievements and abilities if you want to overcome low self-esteem. Never wallow in failures and mistakes since everybody makes mistakes. Learn from your mistakes and move on in life. If you do not know your strengths, learn about them. Sit down and list all your strengths. Use your past experiences to help you do this. Think of the things you can do, the things you know, and past accomplishments you made. When you do this, you realize you have a lot to offer. You can contribute to any situation and can help people in different ways. With this in mind, you become more confident to express your opinions or simply speak up. You have your strengths and values in social situations. The people with the loudest voices and those who appear the most energetic during parties or other social gatherings are not the only ones who contribute to the experience. They may not have something worthwhile to contribute either. Use the following tips to identify your strengths:

Listen to what your well-wishers say about your strengths. They see you quite differently from the way you see yourself. Their advice could give you new insights into your personality.

What are the activities you love to do? What type of work attracts you? What do you enjoy doing? The answers to these questions could give you an idea about your strengths.

CHAPTER SEVENTEEN

IMPROVING YOUR SELF-CONFIDENCE

Your self-confidence can be quite low if you are co-dependent. It prompts you to build your idea of self-worth on materialistic and superficial attributes such as money, prestige, looks, or even success in some aspect of your life. None of these things define what self-confidence means. If your confidence is based on other factors, regardless of whether it is how others perceive you or your perception of what perfection means, it puts you in a precarious state. How will your self-confidence levels be once you have no money, looks, or prestige? Your self-confidence is not based on how well you perform or how others view you. Instead, it is about your belief in yourself. If you start believing that you are only as good as your last performance, you are looking for self-esteem elsewhere and not on the inside. In such a situation, your self-esteem will come and go depending on the circumstances in life.

It can also make you feel quite disconnected from yourself. Self-confidence improves when you can trust yourself and follow your gut. Since co-dependents have a tough time doing both these things, their self-confidence often takes a backseat. If you constantly ask others for their opinions before you do anything or cannot make up your mind, you are giving up your sense of control to someone else. You might not even realize what you are doing, and by the time you do, you end up becoming co-dependent. If you do things for others not because you want to but because you are worried, they will leave you, it will harm your self-confidence. By allowing other's needs and feelings to take priority over yours you start dismissing your own needs and feelings. It creates a lot of internal conflicts and will certainly harm your self-confidence.

Were there any instances in life when you felt that everyone else seems to be super confident about themselves while you were struggling? You might have even started believing that self-confidence is a precious gift only a few are blessed with. Well, you are mistaken if you believe this. What is the secret that others seem to have discovered while you struggle? The secret is quite simple, and it is in your hands. Self-confidence is not an inherent trait. Instead, it is an aspect of your personality that can be improved upon. Self-confidence doesn't have to be something you have, but it can be created. Don't be under the misconception that believing in yourself is synonymous with self-confidence. Instead, self-confidence is a feeling of certainty that you are capable of attaining whatever you concentrate on. Confidence always stems from within, and there are different ways in which you can be more confident in life.

Are You Wondering Why Self-Confidence is Such an Important Quality?

Now, don't be under any misconceptions that self-confidence is the key to solving all problems you face. We all have our bad days and events that upset us. It also doesn't mean you will be sure of yourself. Self-confidence doesn't mean you will know what has to be done. Instead, it helps you trust yourself in all situations. It makes you believe that you can handle whatever curve ball life throws your way. This is an important quality because of life's unpredictability.

Self-confidence is an invaluable asset in all aspects of life; however, there are certain aspects where it is vital, especially when you want to give up. The inclination toward codependency can be overcome with self-confidence. Instead of relying on others for your needs and wants, it makes you believe you are self-sufficient. This increases your confidence to deal with any obstacles you might face. It makes you confident, reliable, and trustworthy. Whether it is your work or personal life, self-confidence cannot be overlooked. If you are not confident about yourself, you will keep second-guessing and doubting everything you think, say, and do. Living life riddled with this self-doubt can make you co-dependent. To break free of this vicious cycle, it is important to concentrate on yourself. If you have a leadership role at work, you need to be confident about your skills and abilities. You should also have the internal belief that you can guide others to achieve their goals.

As mentioned, it is not just your professional life that will improve with self-confidence. The quality of personal relationships is also based on this quality. It allows you to understand your self-worth. It is also a much-needed quality while determining personal boundaries. Without these two things, it is almost impossible to build and maintain healthy and lasting relationships. If you don't believe in yourself, you will knowingly or unknowingly depend on your partner. This instantly shifts the power dynamic and unbalances the relationship. Over a period, it manifests itself as codependency. Self-confidence arms you with the required skills to tackle any personal conflicts too. Apart from it, it is crucial for personal growth and development.

PRINCIPLES OF SELF-CONFIDENCE

If you want to become more confident, you are the only one that can do it. The key to becoming self-confident lies in your hands. The first step is to become willing to change your existing situation. How you think about yourself and personal beliefs, tend to influence how you feel. It, in turn, influences your actions and behaviors. Before learning about becoming self-confident, you need to understand its three primary principles. The three principles of self-confidence are body language, growth mindset, and positivity.

Body Language

Actions always speak louder than words. Why do you think some people are more confident than others? Their actions and behaviors support this assumption. When you are self-confident, it shows. Take some time and think about someone you know who radiates self-confidence. Perhaps it is how they talk, their gestures, or even how they speak about themselves. They probably seem quite self-assured and are not scared of being their true selves. They maintain eye contact, carry themselves confidently, and don't seem like they are second-guessing everything they say.

Do you want to know how to be more confident about yourself? You need to act and behave like you are confident. To improve your self-confidence, you need to concentrate on not just your thoughts; your actions matter too. We not only communicate through our words but also use our body language. From facial expressions to hand gestures and body positioning, there are several important aspects of self-confidence. You will learn more about doing this later in this chapter.

Positivity

An important aspect of self-confidence is positivity. Your general perspective in life matters more than you might have ever considered. Maintaining a positive mindset makes life easier. By changing how you think and focus, you change how you view the world. Instead of getting stuck thinking about all things that can go wrong or the mistakes you have made, it is better to stay positive.

You cannot change the past, and the future is unpredictable. The one thing you have complete control over in life is the present. What you do with the moment right now matters more than what you might have done or what you can do in the future. Instead of dwelling on all things negative, stick to a positive mindset. If you are worried that you will not find a better partner and are stuck in a co-dependent relationship, think about all the good you have in life.

Start working on replacing all the negative beliefs with positive ones. For instance, if you are worried about a presentation at work, don't start thinking about all the things that can go wrong. Is there any point dwelling on all this? Will it increase your productivity? Instead, chances are it will compromise your productivity. If you let this negative thinking guide the way, you might end up transferring the responsibility to someone else. By doing this, you are giving up a good opportunity. What would be a better course of action? Don't waste your precious mental energy, worrying about things you cannot control. Instead, try to do your best and work hard on the presentation. Look for ways to minimize any of the likely obstacles you think you might face. Ask yourself what is the worst that can happen? Once you have the answer, do everything you can to avoid it. Ask yourself what is the best that can happen? Instead of focusing on the negative, concentrate on the positive ones. By changing your focus, it becomes easier to become more self-confident.

Growth Mindset

What, according to you, does confidence include? You probably believe that confidence is a result of prior success. If so, you stop believing that you cannot be confident about yourself unless you are incredibly successful. Perhaps you think that confidence comes when others believe in you. Well, unfortunately, this is not how confidence works. It never stems from others' beliefs. It is based on your thinking and is a core belief. If you are not self-confident, you are sabotaging your chances of success and happiness. Regardless of how successful you are or how much others praise you; you will not truly feel confident unless you start believing in yourself.

Self-confidence doesn't mean you will not make any mistakes, or life will be easy. Instead, it gives you the strength required to accept your mistakes, make the required changes, and move on. When you are self-confident, you start appreciating the effort you make in life instead of focusing solely on the results and outcomes. If you live your life based on whether the outcomes are good or bad, you end up disappointing yourself. If you concentrate on the journey instead of the destination, life becomes more enjoyable. A growth mindset suggests that you believe in your ability to learn and develop. It essentially means you want to grow in life. When you know you can learn and improve yourself, it makes you confident.

TIPS TO BECOME SELF-CONFIDENT

Codependency is not just restricted to personal relationships but can also manifest itself as a dysfunctional relationship at work. Codependency at the workplace can present itself as an extremely controlling or a dominant boss or co-worker who tries to control someone more submissive. Some signs of codependency at the workplace include the constant need for external approval, reduced productivity, low self-esteem, or self-confidence. You might also experience professional burnout because you are stuck in situations you don't want to be in. You might also be scared of speaking up to the domineering boss or co-worker. The good news is, you can reduce this unhealthy codependency by becoming more self-confident in the workplace. In this section, let's look at simple tips you can easily follow to increase your self-confidence in the workplace.

BECOMING MINDFUL OF YOUR BODY LANGUAGE

As mentioned earlier, it is incredibly important to be mindful of your body language. Learn to stand straight, square your shoulders, and do not slouch. Breathe deeply, take purposeful strides while walking, and be brisk. When you maintain a good posture, it makes you feel stronger. It, in turn, increases your self-confidence. Think of someone you know who radiates self-confidence. After this, try to copy their movements and body language. You can use this to gain an edge over others and stand your ground. Where your body goes, the mind certainly follows. Starting immediately, become mindful of your body language. Don't make any gestures or assume positions that make you seem meek, hesitant, or anxious.

Your Achievements Matter

A confident individual knows the importance of his achievements. Yes, it was previously mentioned that self-confidence doesn't stem from your previous success or reduce because of past failures. Learning to take pride in your achievements is an important aspect of being confident. When you take credit for your success and achievements, it shows you value yourself. For instance, if you finally managed to get the promotion you were working hard for, don't brush it off as a stroke of sheer luck. Instead, acknowledge the simple fact that it is your hard work that has paid off. If you managed to do something that benefited someone, take credit for it. You don't have to go out of your way to brag about your success or achievements. Instead, it merely means you are happy with what you do. It also shows you know your capabilities. Most individuals who are co-dependent don't realize the importance of celebrating their achievements. Stop doing this to yourself.

Visualize Your Goals

The human mind is incredibly powerful. Never underestimate all that it is capable of. A positive visualization is a wonderful tool you can use to develop your self-confidence. Believing that you will not succeed or make mistakes is incredibly simple. Most of us tend to have these beliefs. Instead of doing this, you can concentrate on the success you desire to achieve. Visualize your goals, concentrate on the success you want, and make this visualization as clear and detailed as you possibly can. Whenever you start believing you will fail, engage in a little positive visualization. It will increase your self-confidence. If you can visualize the success you want, concentrating on the positive aspects will become easier. It, in turn, will give you the motivation required to keep going.

Appreciating Yourself

Learning to be confident in your body is important. If you are not comfortable in your skin, you end up projecting this discomfort. Over a period, it slowly eats away at your self-confidence. Some of the most popular and incredibly beautiful celebrities have struggled with body image issues. From Arnold Schwarzenegger to Jennifer Lopez, they all struggled to be confident in their skin. Once you are confident within your body, it radiates self-confidence. After all, if you are not comfortable in your skin, how can you ever be confident in any aspect of your life?

The simplest way to do this is by appreciating yourself. Did you ever take a minute to think about all the wonderful things your body does for you? Regardless of what others do for you, your body always works to make your life easier. Don't think of it as a burden and instead rejoice in it because it is a gift. When you look in the mirror, what is the first thing that pops into your head? If all your attention and focus go towards any perceived flaws or self-criticism, stop immediately. You are beautiful the way you are. You don't have to live up to societal notions of beauty.

By accepting your body, the way it is, you start projecting confidence. Once you appreciate your body, you start taking care of it. If you believe there are certain aspects you need to change, do it for yourself. Don't do anything because someone else tells you to or expects it from you. If you notice any internal self-talk based on self-criticism, stop. You are the only one that has the power to do it. No one else can stop you from engaging in negative self-talk.

Whenever you catch yourself criticizing how you look or any flaws you have, stop immediately; once you get used to negative thinking, your brain picks flaws in everything and anything. The only way to change this thinking pattern is by reconditioning it for positivity. By improving your self-talk, you can improve your self-confidence.

The importance of body language was mentioned previously. Take some time, stand in front of a mirror, and observe your general body language. Make a note of your postures, hand gestures, and facial expressions. Do all these things convey self-confidence? Now, look at how self-confident individuals carry themselves. Try mimicking the body language to enhance your self-confidence. You can fake it until you make it. Since these things are well within your control, take action immediately.

Learn to Live in The Moment

A common reason why most of us develop self-limiting beliefs that erode our self-confidence is the inability to live in the moment. Our brains think hundreds of thoughts daily. Some of these thoughts are about the past, some about the future, and others about the present. Take a moment and ask yourself, what will I get out of thinking about the past? Can I change it? What will I get thinking about the future? Will my worries change the future? The answer to all these questions is a solid no. You cannot change the past. You cannot predict the future. Since these two things are completely out of your control, what is the point of letting them guide your present?

If you made any mistakes in the past, forgive yourself. If others have wronged you, forgive them. Learn your lessons from all these instances and improve yourself. Since you have complete control over the present, you can change yourself for the better. If you start worrying about the future, you are living in an imaginary world. There is no guarantee that your worries will materialize. All these worrying thoughts might become a self-fulfilling prophecy if you are not careful.

Whenever you catch yourself doing these things, stop immediately. Think about all the different steps and actions you can do today to change your life. You can shape your future according to your desires if you start living in the present. By living in the moment, you become more self-confident. By decluttering your mind off all these unnecessary thoughts, you can direct your mental energies toward something more productive and constructive. You can work on creating the future you desire.

Start Loving Yourself

A common reason for codependency is certain people are incapable of loving themselves. Before you expect love from others, learn to love yourself. If you don't love yourself, how can you expect it from anyone else? Unconsciously, you might have developed several limiting beliefs that are preventing you from understanding your true worth. Take some time and make a note of all your accomplishments and achievements. Regardless of whether they are small or big, they are a victory. Rejoice in these victories. Make a note of all your positive traits and accept them.

The chances of getting stuck in co-dependent relationships increase if you don't love yourself. Your self-worth and the ability to love yourself determine your self-confidence. Once you start loving yourself, you become more confident about who you are. When you are confident of this, you are not scared of being your true self. This change in attitude will reflect on every aspect of your life.

Think About Exciting Things

Up until now, all of the different tips mentioned were focused on how to change your mindset to increase confidence. There are several other useful and practical techniques you can incorporate into your daily routine to become even more self-confident. One such thing is to think of things that excite you. If you worry or are unsure about a specific circumstance, you can think about your recent accomplishments. Perhaps you can think of something that motivates and excites you. By doing this, you are not dwelling on the negative and are focusing on the positive. It secures that you feel more confident about yourself.

Learn to Make and Maintain Eye Contact

Eye contact is one of the simplest yet most effective ways to project self-confidence. Eyes are the windows to one's soul. If you are not confident, it shows in your inability to maintain eye contact. By maintaining eye contact, you show confidence as well as find it easier to connect with others. Whenever you communicate, maintain eye contact for at least 80% of the conversation. Don't make it obvious to the extent that you don't blink. If you don't blink at all, it makes you seem too intense and can make the other person incredibly uncomfortable.

Learning to Say No

Another practical tip you can use to increase your self-confidence is by learning to say no. This is one useful skill that comes in handy in all aspects of your life. When you say no, it means you are aware of your boundaries. If the inner voice tells you that one of these boundaries is violated, you need to listen to it. You are not disappointing others by saying no. Instead, you are merely respecting yourself. It also teaches you to prioritize what matters and doesn't in life. You can effectively prevent yourself from getting stuck in situations that you could have easily avoided if you say no. It will take some time and effort to become fully comfortable with saying no. It might not even come naturally to you. With practice, you can build your self-confidence by doing this. It also increases your overall sense of wellbeing. Here are some great tips on how to say no:

Simply say no without beating around the bush. Don't try to find excuses to say no. Many times, especially for those who have taken you for granted, just saying no upfront is the best way to handle it. Don't think it might be rude. It's just being honest.

You can be assertive, even while being courteous. If your pushy partner is insisting that you don't go out with your friends but stay home instead, tell him, "I am sorry I cannot listen to you. I have promised my friends I will come, and I hate to break promises." Then go and meet your friends.

Set boundaries. Let people know when your boundaries are being crossed. Don't hesitate to tick off repeat offenders.

The worst thing about saying no for the first time, especially in a codependent relationship, is that the other person will not accept it easily. He or she is bound to compel you to do what he or she wants. It is imperative that you stand firm on your decision to say no. You get it right the first time; you will notice it gets easier the second time.

If you cannot say no, others will take you for granted. If you don't want others to walk all over you, you need to stand up for yourself. Whether it is a domineering co-worker or a controlling partner, it doesn't matter as long as you can say no. Co-dependent individuals often struggle with this.

The tips and techniques given in this chapter are simple to follow and implement. Most of them can be easily incorporated into your daily routine. It will take time and effort to consciously incorporate them initially. After a while, they will come naturally to you. Be patient with yourself, and you will see a positive change. Once you are self-confident, it becomes easier to avoid any form of codependency.

CHAPTER EIGHTEEN

HOW TO OVERCOME INSECURITIES

It is almost impossible to find someone who doesn't have any insecurity. The only difference is, some are better at hiding or dealing with them than others. We are all guilty of worrying about what others think about us; for example, whether we're good looking, or if we are doing what we are supposed to do. We also worry about failure and failing others. There are different things we are constantly insecure about. Added to this is the world of social media we live in. This culture of social media has conditioned us to seek approval from external sources, so it is important to overcome insecurities.

If you are constantly overwhelmed by insecurities, you are not living the life you are supposed to. Instead, you are living in a constant state of comparison. You are worrying about whether you will live up to the image of perfection you have created in your mind. Unfortunately, perfection is nothing more than a mirage. Stop chasing it, and instead, concentrate on living your life to the fullest.

When you are riddled with insecurities, you are not confident about yourself. This lack of confidence and insecurities can make you codependent. Whether it is a controlling coworker or a domineering partner, these insecurities prevent you from seeing your true self. It also increases the chances of settling for less than what you deserve. Unless you are confident in your skin and know how to deal with your insecurities, you cannot go after what you want.

For instance, you might be in a relationship with someone because you are certain that you will not find anyone who will accept you the way you are. You are insecure about yourself, and it prevents you from cultivating and maintaining healthy and lasting relationships. Since relationships are important in every aspect, not creating the right ones can be a major setback. If you believe you are not good enough, it slowly damages your self-esteem, self-confidence, and self-worth.

Now, you might be wondering how you can get over these insecurities. The answer is quite simple. You need to make peace with yourself. To do this, you must be willing to face all that you've been avoiding so far. It takes a lot of courage and effort. The result will truly be worth every little step you take. To overcome your insecurities, you need to first understand and acknowledge them. Unless you do this, you cannot tackle them. If you keep ignoring or avoiding them, they become stronger. Don't do this to yourself. You deserve better and don't settle for less than what you deserve.

OBSTACLES THAT RESULT IN INSECURITIES

The power to overcome your insecurities lies in your hands. If that's the case, what is preventing you? In this section, let's look at some common obstacles most face. These are often in the form of old wounds that never truly healed. Unless you do this, chances of finding yourself in codependent relationships over and over increase. Life has a funny way of teaching us lessons we refuse to learn. It constantly puts you in situations where it is trying to teach you something you've been refusing to learn. Once you learn these lessons, you can move on.

Criticism

One of the leading causes of insecurities is criticism. Whether it is a parent, relative, or a loved one who criticized you when you were growing up, chances are you have managed to internalize it. If you have been criticized during your childhood, you end up accepting these criticisms as the absolute truth. Even more so if they are from someone you love, respect, and care about. These criticisms might stay in your head long after the events have gone by. The chances are that others criticized you because of certain insecurities they have. Their criticism was nothing more than a manifestation of their insecurities. You might have not even realized that you have internalized every criticism you faced in life. Over a period, these criticisms become strong beliefs that prevent you from seeing yourself the way you are. When you are loved, accepted, and respected unconditionally, it builds your self-confidence. The lack of these things prevents you from developing true confidence. Instead, you start constantly worrying about what others might think or believe.

Developing A Negative Self-Image

Your self-image matters a lot. It shows what you think and feels about yourself. If it is negative, your perspective towards life will be riddled with negativity. It can also be a reason for the insecurities you harbor. Being criticized excessively can result in a negative self-image. The image you have created about yourself in your mind tends to guide your perspective towards yourself and life in general. If you believe you are incompetent, a failure, or unable to do anything on your own, you start acting on these beliefs. Your actions are a result of your thoughts. If your thoughts are predominantly negative, your actions also take on this hue.

A Constant Need for Approval

Most individuals in codependent relationships have a constant need for approval. They seek disapproval from external sources. Unless they get this approval, they don't feel worthy of themselves. If you live your life looking for this approval from others, you are not true to yourself. You might also change yourself to the extent that you no longer know who you are. The need for approval creates an extreme internal conflict that prevents you from being your true self. It turns you into a codependent individual who fears disapproval.

Lack of Trust

A common reason for the insecurities we harbor is the fear of abandonment or rejection. It stems from a basic lack of trust.

When you don't believe that someone else will be by your side and accept you the way you are, it makes you insecure. You lack the trust that someone else will be fine with all this and see your side of things. If you believe this, sooner or later turns into a fear of abandonment or rejection. You end up becoming incredibly insecure about who you are. You might also create a facade to make sure that others will accept you. By doing this, you are merely strengthening the insecurities you have. This kind of thinking increases the risk of codependency.

Constant Comparison

Social media and the media dominate the world we live in. We are constantly flooded by images, videos, and snippets from the lives of people who seem to have it all. It seems as if everyone has figured out the key to perfection. When these things constantly surround you, the comparison starts. If you keep comparing yourself to others, it increases your self-doubt and creates dissatisfaction. It also makes you insecure about the life you have and who you are.

Lack of Self-Approval

The lack of self-approval is also a source of insecurities. When you put all the above-mentioned factors together, it becomes incredibly difficult to accept oneself. Due to this, you start rejecting a significant part of whom you are. Believe it or not, everyone has insecurities, and even the ones you think are perfect can believe they're not. If you don't approve of yourself, you are essentially distancing from your inner self. Instead of embracing your inner persona, you start looking for external sources of approval. If you don't accept your insecurities, you cannot work on them. Without self-approval, you live in a constant state of denial. By living in denial, you are effectively sabotaging any chances of growth and happiness in life.

Do any of these obstacles sound familiar to you? It might seem like there is a lot to overcome. You have the power to do all this. You can fight all your insecurities and move forward in life. Try to understand that the only person standing in your way is you.

Dealing with Insecurities

You can overcome all of the obstacles that are preventing you from tackling your insecurities. The only way to do this is by going through them. The obstacles are essentially showing you the path towards tackling any insecurity you harbor. By embracing them and working with them, you can figure a way out. Don't think of your insecurities as a failure. Every obstacle or insecurity is nearly a chance to improve. In this section, let's look at simple tips you can follow to overcome your insecurities.

Your insecurities might have been shaped if you were criticized in the past by authority figures in your life. If so, the first step in learning to let go of the past is to understand where and who the insecurity stems from, and the second step is to forgive them. There's no point and holding onto all those. Try to understand that their criticism was the manifestation of their insecurities they might not have even been aware of. Their inability to struggle with their inner demons made them extremely critical of you. Their imperfect behavior was far from desirable or correct. Learning to forgive them aids you in letting go of any resentment. By acknowledging that the criticism was baseless, it becomes easier to repair your self-belief.

Now, it's time for a little self-assessment. Make a note of all the different aspects of your life you are not happy about. Make a note of different parts of your body and inner self that you are insecure about. Look at all your imperfections and ask, "Are they as bad as I seem to think?" The chances are that upon closer inspection, you'll realize you are extremely critical of yourself.

If you don't accept yourself the way you are, don't expect it from anyone else. If a friend or a loved one came to you and the roles were reversed, what would your advice be? Why don't you start following the loving advice you would have handed out?

Apart from accepting yourself, you also need to approve yourself. A defining trait of codependency is the desire for approval from others. If you look for attention and approval from external sources, catch yourself in the moment, and stop. Instead of depending on external sources, this approval needs to come from within. You need to approve of yourself. Not desiring approval from others doesn't mean you don't want to make any connections. Instead, it means that you love and accept yourself how you are. You finally realize that you are all you need.

It might be difficult but resist the urge to compare others to you. A simple fact you need to understand is what you see doesn't always portray the entire story. The world of social media we live in only allows others to post snippets from their lives. Most of these snippets tend to be quite close to perfection. Now, these are just snippets and not the entire story. What is the point of constantly comparing yourself? Especially when you realize that you don't even know what is happening behind the scenes. We all have our struggles and demons to deal with. Even all those with seemingly perfect lives are far from it. Instead of comparing yourself with others, look inward. The only person you need to compare yourself with is you. Try to be a better version of yourself. Comparing apples and oranges leads to nothing good. Instead of believing that something is lacking in your life, acknowledge all the good that exists.

CHAPTER NINETEEN

SIMPLE TIPS TO LET GO OF FEARS

We all have certain fears in life. It is a basic human tendency. If these fears are preventing you from living your life to the fullest, it is time to eliminate them. Whether it is the fear that you will not find someone who loves and accepts you unconditionally or the fear of showing your true self, it is time to let him or her go. When left unregulated, these fears can manifest themselves as tendencies leaning toward codependency. In this section, let's look at some simple and practical tips you can follow to overcome fears in your life.

Make A Note of Your Fears

The only way to overcome your fears is by acknowledging them. If you keep avoiding or ignoring them, how can you tackle them? Whatever you fear, acknowledge it without any judgment. It is best to acknowledge if you are scared you will not find a good partner or that you cannot accomplish anything good in life. Since this fear is holding you back, acknowledge it, and let it go.

Dig Deeper

Make a list of all the things that matter to you in life. After this, make a list of all the likely hurdles or obstacles you face in these aspects. By doing this, you get a better understanding of your fears. You might think you cannot do this. You can do it, and all it takes is a little courage. It is okay to be scared and perfectly normal to worry about different outcomes in life. Try to understand why you are not taking action in certain aspects of your life. What are the reasons for this? While doing this, live only in the moment and don't worry about whatever has happened in the past.

Time to Analyze the Fear

Now that you are aware of your fears, it is time to analyze them. If you have a long list, start dealing with them one fear at a time. What are you afraid of? Why are you afraid of it? Do you believe that if you don't succeed, it means you have failed? Why does failure scare you? What, according to you, does failure mean? How did others treat you when you failed in the past?

By answering these questions, you can understand your attitude towards the fears you harbor. Unknowingly, certain past circumstances and events might have conditioned your brain and tricked it to firmly hold onto some fears. If your attitude and experience towards certain events are negative, you need to change it. If a child is praised and loved only when he does something the parent desires, it creates a fear of failure. After all, the parents' affection and love are withheld unless he succeeds. It can even make him scared of making mistakes. These fears tend to stay with him even in adulthood. He believes that unless he does everything perfectly, he will not be loved or accepted.

Instead, it is better to accept that making mistakes is a part of life. The only thing you need to do is concentrate on learning from those mistakes and become better. Do this because you want to grow and not because of what others expect. By rationally analyzing your fears, you finally get a chance to determine whether these fears are based on reality or not. If the fare is not realistic, what is the point of holding onto it?

Change Your Point of View

It is time to face your fears since you are now aware of what your fears are and where they stem from. Ask yourself whether your fear is real. The next aspect is to see what will happen if you fail? If you don't even take the first step, you will be left wondering, "what if?" If you don't want to live your life riddled with what-ifs, it's time to change your perspective of the fear. Once you change your attitude about the fear, facing it becomes easier. For instance, if you are scared that you will not be enough, ask yourself why you think so. If you think you will not find a partner who unconditionally loves and accepts you the way you are, asks why do you think this will happen?

Make a list of your opinions about why you think you are not good enough the way you are. Also, make a note of your reasons if you think you will not find the partner you deserve. Once you have the reasons, ask yourself what will happen if you don't succeed the first time around? The answer is nothing will happen. Don't be critical or judgmental of yourself while writing down your answers. Instead, let the words flow. You can analyze it later. By doing this, understanding why you should not hold on to these fears. If you desire to grow, letting go of negativity is important. Perspective matters more than anything else. By shifting your perspective towards something more positive, overcoming your fears becomes easier.

An Alternative Plan

If you are worried that you will never find someone who will love and accept you unconditionally, look for an alternate plan. What will happen if you are single? Nothing will happen. Instead of concentrating on the negative aspects, try to understand that you get a better chance at understanding yourself. By falling in love with yourself first, you become adept at tackling your fears. What if you don't get the promotion you've been working hard for? You might feel bad, but it is not the end of the world. Sooner or later, your hard work will pay off. Instead of trying to live your life according to societal expectations or worrying about what others might think or feel, concentrate on yourself. There are plenty of opportunities in life. You cannot make the most of them if you don't act on them.

Once you let go of any rational fears that are preventing you from excelling in life and finding happiness, you get a better understanding of yourself. You will know what you want or don't want and the reasons for the same. This reduces codependency.

CHAPTER TWENTY

EMBRACE THE IDEA OF SELF-CARE

Taking care of yourself needs to be a priority. You are the only one capable of doing this. It is not selfish to prioritize self-care. Instead, it is a sign of self-respect and self-love. If you don't care for yourself, how can you care for anyone else? If you constantly look for external sources to fulfill this need, you are setting yourself up for disappointment. If all your time, effort, and energy go towards taking care of other's needs, you will be left with nothing for yourself. This is one of the reasons why people end up in codependent relationships. Follow these tips to start making self-care a priority.

Let Go of Overthinking

Think of life as an adventure. You don't need a plan for everything. Stop worrying about searching for answers to all of life's questions immediately. Instead, it is a journey that slowly unfolds. By overthinking, you are merely increasing the frustration you experience at any given point. It is pointless. It is important to understand the consequences of your actions, but overthinking prevents you from taking the first step. You end up getting stuck in your head. Enjoy life, stop overthinking, and take action. If you make mistakes, you can fix it later. If you don't take any action, you will never get anywhere.

Accept Reality

There are certain aspects of life you can control and plenty that are beyond your responsibility of control. What is the point of obsessing over the things that are beyond your control? Apart from increasing the stress, you experience; it does not add any value to your life. So, let them go. Accept the reality of life and start living in the moment. Take a deep breath and give yourself a break. You don't have to control everything or everyone. Instead, focus all these energies on your inner self. Start doing things that you love.

Take A Break

Life can be quite hectic. We constantly live in an overstimulated environment. Due to this, we forget about the beauty of the life we have right now. Take a break from your busy life and head outdoors. Spend some time in nature and appreciate the stillness. This is not only meditative but also incredibly therapeutic. By taking regular breaks, you are reenergizing your body and mind for the challenges that lie ahead.

Avoid Comparison

Stop comparing yourself with others. Who you are is the only thing that matters? What you do with the time right now will create a lasting impact on your life. When you live your life in a constant state of comparison, you will be dissatisfied with all the good you have. It also encourages you to focus on everything that is missing. Over a period, you will develop a lacking attitude. What is the point of all this? So, stop comparing and live your life how you want to. You are your true competitor. Try to be a better version of yourself. Compare yourself with the person you were, are, and want to be.

Do Things That Scare You

Codependency might be preventing you from enjoying life to the fullest. There might be several things you are scared of. These fears aren't always rational. However, they are effectively preventing you from living your life how you're supposed to. If you don't want to wake up one fine day and wonder where it went, it's time to take action. Make it a point to do at least one thing you are scared of daily. Perhaps you are scared of public speaking, meeting with strangers, or your insecurities. Whatever it is, work on them. It's the only thing you can do. It also guarantees that you are heading in the right direction. Every fear you overcome increases your self-confidence.

Hold on to Your True Friends

Relationships matter a lot in life. The company you keep influences your overall personality and attitude. Take some time and analyze all the relationships in your life. Happy and positive relationships are the ones that make you feel better about yourself and motivate you to do better. If a relationship doesn't add any value to your life, let it go. Don't let codependency prevent you from doing this. Holding on to toxic relationships merely drains your happiness and joy. Nothing is better than nonsense. Toxicity has no place in your life. Understand and accept this. Once you declutter your relationships, you are making more space for happier ones. By holding on to your true friends, the ones who have seen you at your absolute worst and have motivated you to do better, cherish them. Spend more time with your loved ones.

Acknowledge Your Strengths

Your inner critic might constantly remind you of your weaknesses and flaws. This negative internal dialogue conditions your mind for negativity. Instead of dwelling on your weaknesses, acknowledge and accept all your strengths. By doing this, you're focusing on something better. Remind yourself of your strengths every day. It reduces codependency and increases your self-confidence. By acknowledging your strengths, you become self-reliant. Self-reliance is a great way to break free of codependency. Once you acknowledge your strengths, you can improve them. You can also use them to attain your goals and dreams.

Pay Attention to Your Diet

You might not have given it much conscious thought, but your diet plays an important role in your overall health and wellbeing. What you feed your body determines an important aspect of your life—physical health. If you are physically fit and strong, you automatically feel better about yourself. If you have any insecurities about your looks, pay attention to your diet, and add some exercise to your daily routine. Do these things because you want to improve yourself and not because of others' expectations.

Start Exercising Regularly

Exercise is a great stress buster. Whenever you exercise, feel-good hormones known as endorphins are produced. They counteract the harmful effects of serotonin, a stress-inducing hormone. If you are stressed, worried, or riddled with negative thoughts, take a break, and go for a walk. Even something as simple as jogging every day for 20 minutes will make you feel better about yourself.

Stand Up for Yourself

Try to understand the difference between being nice to others and letting them take you for granted. If you let others take you for granted, it reduces your self-esteem, self-worth, and self-confidence. None of these things are desirable for personal growth. By standing up for yourself, you can break free of codependency. It also shows your inner strength. No one else can or will do this for you. So, take a stand for all that you believe in. Once you start living your life based on your core values, it reduces internal conflict and turmoil. It also points you in the right direction. By taking a stand for yourself, you prevent others from taking you for granted. It increases your self-confidence and makes you more assured.

Practice Forgiveness

Learning to forgive might seem like a simple concept, but it is quite difficult to implement. If you have discovered that you have codependent tendencies, you might be upset with yourself. This realization might also make you resent others. All this resentment merely increases dissatisfaction. Nothing good will ever come out of holding onto these resentments and frustrations. Instead, acknowledge whatever has happened, learn your lessons, and move on. By forgiving yourself and others who have wronged you, your misery reduces. Forgiveness is important to grow and move on.

Practice Gratitude

By practicing gratitude daily, you are not only taking care of yourself but are acknowledging all the good in your life. By showing gratitude for everything you love and cherish, you are attracting more of this desirable energy. Take a moment and think about the different things you are grateful for. It can be something as simple as the realization that there is some scope for improvement in your life. Now that you have understood this, you finally have the power to make the required changes.

CONCLUSION

Let us start this concluding chapter with this beautiful thought, "Look at the mirror. Love what you see and start the love affair with yourself from this point onwards." This is, perhaps, the first and the most difficult step to take in your life. But once you have done this, your path of recovery will be smooth because no one can replace YOU in your life and in this world.

Here is a beautiful Zen story to teach you about how each of us is unique and beautiful. A warrior went to a Zen master and said to him, "I have helped so many people with my warrior skills. I have defended and protected the weak. I am proud of my achievements. And yet, when I see you in such a calm state, I feel my achievements have no significance."

The Zen master took the warrior outside and showed him the night sky, where the moon was shining brightly. The master said, "See how beautiful and bright the moon is! It will soon cross the sky and make way for the sun, which is way brighter. But does the moon complain about not being as bright as the sun?"

"No, it doesn't," continued the Zen master. "Because each element of this universe is unique and has its own purpose of fulfilling."

Remind yourself you are beautiful and unique. You have a purpose that no one else can fulfill, and that purpose is to lead your life on your terms. Don't allow someone else's desires get in the way of your dreams. You are the master of your destiny. If things are happening to you, it is because you are allowing them to happen. If people are treating you badly, then it is because you are allowing people to do so.

Remind yourself not to give in to mean and nasty people. You deserve happiness and joy. If others don't give it to you, then you reach out and take it from the world.

If you are codependent and want to find a way to overcome these behaviors, you can use this book as your guide. This book provides all the information you need about codependency. You will learn about the different behaviors you exhibit if you are codependent. The book also has tips and techniques to help you in your recovery process.

You develop other behaviors if you are codependent, and the book provides information on how you can overcome those issues. You will gather information about what negative self-talk is and how you can overcome it. The most important thing to remember is that you need to remain positive if you want to change the way you and the people around you perceive you. You also need to find a way to care for yourself. This book leaves you with some tips you can use to care for yourself and overcome your insecurities. If you want to remain happy and maintain a positive outlook on life, you should learn to let go of negativity.

Use the tips in the book to change the way you look at life. It is important to note that a positive outlook helps you deal with any situation in life. Thank you for purchasing the book. I hope you got the information you are looking for.

REFERENCES

4 Ways to Stop Beating Yourself Up, Once and For All. (n.d.). Psychology Today website: https://www.psychologytoday.com/intl/blog/living-forward/201603/4-ways-stop-beating-yourself-once-and-all

8 Common Causes of Low Self-Esteem. (, 2014). Goodchoicesgoodlife.org website: http://www.goodchoicesgoodlife.org/choices-for-young-people/boosting-self-esteem/

9 Signs of Low Self-Esteem & 10 Ways Grow Confidence. (2019, May 18). The Couch: A Therapy & Mental Wellness Blog website: https://blog.zencare.co/boost-self-esteem/

10 Types of Negative Self-Talk (and How to Correct Them) | Nick Wignall. (2018, July 27). Nick Wignall website: https://nickwignall.com/negative-self-talk/

Berry, J. (2017, October 31). Codependent relationships: Symptoms, warning signs, and behavior. www.medicalnewstoday.com website: https://www.medicalnewstoday.com/articles/319873

Byrne, M., Edmundson, R., & Rankin, E. D. (2005). Symptom Reduction and Enhancement of Psychosocial Functioning

Utilizing a Relational Group Treatment Program for Dependent/Codependent Population. Alcoholism Treatment Quarterly, 23(4), 69–84. https://doi.org/10.1300/j020v23n04_05

Cherry, K. (2010, July 20). What Exactly Is Self-Esteem? Verywell Mind website: https://www.verywellmind.com/what-is-self-esteem-2795868

Codependents Anonymous - 12-Step Codependency Support Group. (2013, May 6). Recovery.org website: https://www.recovery.org/support-groups/codependents-anonymous/

Codependency Myths. (2019, July 12). The Recovery Village Drug and Alcohol Rehab website: https://www.therecoveryvillage.com/mental-health/codependency/related/codependency-myths/

Codependency Treatment and Information. (n.d.). Treatment Solutions website: https://www.treatmentsolutions.com/programs-for/codependency/

Firestone, L. (2017, June 5). Low Self-Esteem: What Does it Mean to Lack Self-Esteem? PsychAlive website: https://www.psychalive.org/low-self-esteem

Hambrick, B. (n.d.). 3 Types of Codependency | Brad Hambrick. http://bradhambrick.com/3-types-of-codependency/

Knudson, T. M., & Terrell, H. K. (2012). Codependency, Perceived Interparental Conflict, and Substance Abuse in the

Family of Origin. The American Journal of Family Therapy, 40(3), 245–257. https://doi.org/10.1080/01926187.2011.610725

Lancer, D. (2016, May 17). Recovery from Codependency. psychcentral.com website: https://psychcentral.com/lib/recovery-from-codependency/

Lancer, D. (2018, October 8). Symptoms of Codependency. Psych Central website: https://psychcentral.com/lib/symptoms-of-codependency/

Morin, A. (2020, September 28). How to Get Help for Relationship Addiction. Verywell Mind website: https://www.verywellmind.com/what-s-the-best-codependency-treatment-5070487

Robbins, T. (2019). How to Be Confident, 3 Easy Tips to Transform Your Confidence Today. tonyrobbins.com website: https://www.tonyrobbins.com/building-confidence/how-to-be-confident/

Selva, J. (2018, February 9). Codependency: What Are The Signs & How To Overcome It. PositivePsychology.com website: https://positivepsychology.com/codependency-definition-signs-worksheets/

Scott, E. (2020, February 25). How to Reduce Negative Self-Talk for a Better Life. Verywell Mind website: https://www.verywellmind.com/negative-self-talk-and-how-it-affects-us-4161304

Ward, D. (2019, May 7). 10 ways to overcome low self-esteem. Psychologies website: https://www.psychologies.co.uk/10-ways-overcome-low-self-esteem

https://www.psychologytoday.com/us/blog/focus-forgiveness/201105/the-hawaiian-secret-forgiveness#:~:text=The%20Hawaiian%20word%20ho'oponopono,to%20whom%20we%20are%20connected.